the house that jill built

the house that jill built

A Woman's Guide to Home Building

JUDY OSTROW

Photographs by Karen Leffler

GIBBS SMITH

Gibbs Smith, Publisher
Salt Lake City

First Edition
09 08 07 06 05 5 4 3 2 1

Published by
Gibbs Smith, Publisher
P.O. Box 667
Layton, Utah 84041

Orders: 1.800.748.5439
www.gibbs-smith.com

Designed by Dawn DeVries Sokol
Printed and bound in Hong Kong
"Woman's Touch" and "The Little Poem" from *Covering Rough Ground* by Kate Braid, published in 1991 by Polestar, an imprint of Raincoast Books.

Library of Congress Cataloging-in-Publication Data
Ostrow, Judy.
The house that Jill built : a woman's guide to home building / Judy Ostrow ; photography by Karen Leffler.— 1st ed.
p. cm.
ISBN 1-58685-459-3
1. Log cabins—United States—Design and construction—Anecdotes. 2. House construction—United States—Anecdotes. 3. Women construction workers—United States—Anecdotes. I. Leffler, Karen. II. Title.

TH4840.088 2004
690'.837—dc22
2004023127

Safety first. Using tools improperly can cause injury, or even death. Do not perform tasks you are unsure about. Follow manufacturers' instructions for any tool you use.

To my father, William Gilbert Platt,
who let me hold the toolbox
and gifted me with a lifelong curiosity
about how buildings are made.

contents

introduction

"Building a house is something like psycho-analysis. You don't know what emotions will float to the surface, or what memories will be stirred up, and you do learn about yourself!"

— LISA HAWKINS

THE INSPIRATION FOR THIS BOOK came from many places. A personal longing for competence with tools and a lifelong love of houses were its genesis. Then, a workshop about designing and building one's own home – where I found myself in a classroom, surrounded by a dozen other women with the same interest – popped the book's title out of the universe of ideas and into my mind on the drive home. I just had to run with it.

I found myself up late at night, searching on the Internet for leads – women who'd already built their houses, who were willing to share the experience. I told everybody about my idea; some who took it seriously gave me names and numbers. Gradually, I found the wonderful people whose work is chronicled in these pages. As we conversed, in face-to-face meetings, by phone and e-mail, I grew to understand something important.

So many home design books deal exclusively with the end product – a picture-perfect haven. Far fewer document the journey – that long process between inspiration and pillow fluffing that constitutes the growth, learning and self-affirmation that come from a project so large, one that is still thought of as non-traditional for women. I decided to make this book an exception.

In these pages, we'll visit ten women who took on this journey for themselves. I asked each of the ten homeowners to really think about her own unique process: where she got the idea, how she developed the skills, who helped her, what were the struggles and the victories, and how she feels now. Each of them sat down and wrote their answers back to me. So each of the first ten chapters is far more than pretty pictures and explanatory captions. We get to share the ride. For this, I bow to all the homeowners for their openness and generosity with time and spirit.

Over the course of three summers, five classes of women, including the author's, built this cabin on the Yestermorrow campus.

And then, to be up for this task, I learned, by attempting them myself, the skills my subjects had struggled with.

If I Were a Carpenter, and a Lady

Learning to wield a hammer and operate a table saw were never part of my early education. My all-female high school offered no technical courses that might have helped these skills along. Back then, it was an unwritten law: tools were for guys.

My dad, a gifted amateur carpenter, let me watch as he labored in his workshop, making all kinds of furnishings for our house. I loved going to lumberyards with him, inhaling the scent of newly cut two-by-fours. I handed him the tools as he poured the foundation and then framed and built a new kitchen for my mother. It never occurred to my father to let me work beside him. A girl in the 1950s just didn't do those things. But my eyes-only training in construction left me with an unscratched itch to work with wood and nails.

Finally, in 2002, I got my opportunity. Looking for other women who had the same itch as mine, and wanting to make their stories into this book, I signed up for a class in carpentry for women at Yestermorrow Design/Build School — with female instructors who are also building professionals. I was on my way.

Arriving at the school in Vermont on a Sunday afternoon in July, I met my fellow classmates: a high school math teacher from central Texas, two hospice nurses from California,

Carpentry student/architecture intern Anya Raredon drew a detailed elevation for the cabin's facade.

Cathy and her partners (one is shown in the "before" photo) have given their first investment a new roof, porch, and paint job. Next comes the interior.

a woman from Maine who had already designed and worked on three of her own houses, an attorney and mother of five from Ohio, a young woman from Houston who spent several months a year as chief purser on oil tankers around the globe, and a young undergraduate intern from the Yale School of Architecture.

The teachers, two women of gentle and friendly demeanor, set us at ease with their goals: to be safe, to learn lots of new skills, and to have a good time. Their expertise was also comforting; each had worked as a carpenter for more than twenty years, and both had built their own homes (see chapters 4 and 6). But none of the students were quite sure of what we'd be capable of learning.

In five days we were transformed.

While the physical proof of our work was obvious — we had sided a cabin, installed its windows and secured the platform for its deck — the inner work we had done was even more gratifying.

- The mystique of the quilting bee, the sewing circle, the church supper — all traditional feminine pastimes — applies equally to a building team of women. In our work, we established a beautiful bond, helped each other and made a fine result that pleased us all.
- Using power equipment (the scariest idea for most of us) is just like any other new skill. Learn the rules, respect what the tool can do and ask for help when you think you need it. It's not brain surgery — and women have been doing *that* for years. Once you understand the tools, you realize that the power is *you.*
- So much of so-called women's work is invisible; our cooking is consumed, the well-swept floor gets dirty in no time, the laundry is destined for the hamper even as it is put away, clean and folded, in the drawers. By contrast, building leaves sturdy, permanent evidence of what you've been doing all day. And the evidence makes you feel really good about yourself.

Carpentry students Laurie and Tracy completed a strawbale house in the West Virginia mountains in the spring of 2004.

I recently wrote my fellow carpentry class graduates to find out what they were doing with their new skills and confidence. It was gratifying to hear how much that week meant to everyone.

The Ohio attorney, Gigi Fried, is building a new house with her husband, and recently went back to our school for a design course that will help her direct the construction.

The mystique of the quilting bee, the sewing circle, the church supper — all traditional feminine pastimes — applies equally to a building team of women.

After retiring from her career as a math teacher, Joan Blankenship and her husband continue to buy properties for investment, renovating and sprucing them up for rental. When she replied to my note, Joan was preparing to tackle another house. She's hoping to go back to carpentry class to develop more skills.

The merchant marine/oil tanker purser, Cathy Hays, has found a new direction for her time when she's on dry land. Teaming up with two partners, she's now begun a business renovating houses in Fredericksburg, Texas — a tourist mecca in that state's lovely hill country — turning old and tired-looking structures into charming bed-and-breakfast inns.

The California hospice nurses, Laurie Ardison and Tracy Vaughan, stayed on at the school that summer to take another course. They have just completed a beautiful strawbale house that they designed, contracted and worked on themselves in the West Virginia mountains. The local carpenters they hired had never seen a house like the one the women wanted to build. "They were wonderful," says Laurie. "Until things really got going, it was an act of faith — for them, and for us too. But we did it!" I hear happy victory in her voice.

The woman from Maine, Lisa Hawkins, has finished her home. You can see the results in chapter 7.

Anya Raredon, the Yale architecture intern, has graduated and now works for an architectural firm in central Vermont — the Edgcomb Design Group — not far from the Yestermorrow school.

This book is the result of what I've been doing, in addition to acting as general contractor for a kitchen rehab at my home in suburban New York. Both are as complete as I can make them.

true tales of home making

HOMEBUILDING CAN BE A MIND-AND-BODY-WRENCHING EXPERIENCE. In fact, it's a little like having a baby. Both events start with an idea — a dream, really.

Once the dream becomes a doable thing, then you have to wait and wait and wait for the reward. Along with anticipation, there are moments of nausea, big and unexpected changes in appearance, and terror that the whole process will never end. But just as nature rewards a woman for all her labor with a beautiful child, the building process also ends — eventually — with a great new space.

The funny thing is, when a woman finally holds her baby in her arms, she forgets all the ugly stuff. It's nature's gift to women, this memory lapse. It's also nature's insurance policy that we might be inclined to repeat the experience.

A similar, mystical amnesia also extends to people who build and renovate. When everything is finally cleaned up, freshly painted and ready for the decorative details, we've just about forgotten what it took to get there. Sometimes, we're willing to try it again — just not right away, please.

"From little ideas, great things can develop." Homeowner/designer/builder Lisa Hawkins carved a niche in one wall of her strawbale home to display a treasure — the seed from a giant redwood, an amazingly small genesis for this massive tree. It reminds her daily to nurture her dreams.

Siobhan Daggett

SOUTHERN COMFORT, NEW ENGLAND STYLE

"I drew for six days — floor plans, elevations, interior details. This was the beginning of the process."

Siobhan siding the house, twenty feet up.

"WE LIVED IN OUR FIRST HOME — a condominium — for fifteen years. A friend of mine who worked in real estate encouraged me to look into buying land and building a house," says Siobhan Dagget. "She assured me that we could have our own place for what we were already paying on our mortgage and condo fees. My father-in-law, who was very ill, also was insistent that my husband and I have a home and property of our own.

"On New Year's Eve 1999, everything seemed to come together. I got out my drafting table and some pencils, and started drawing. I already had a picture in my mind, as we had looked through lots of plan books and all of us — my husband, John, daughter, Tara, and I — had agreed on the style of house we wanted. From a 2- by 3-inch thumbnail sketch that we'd found in a library book, I drew the entire house in ½-inch scale, modifying as I went to better suit my ideas. I drew for six days — floor plans, elevations, interior details. This was the beginning of the process."

space: 4,600 square feet • **best deal:** marble counters in the baths, marble hearth and fireplace surrounds — all remnants; saved a pile of money • **time to complete:** 6 months • **key accomplishments:** installing my own kitchen, siding the house, staying married!

Siobhan uses graceful archways and columns to define space in the public rooms, as well as in important private spaces, such as the master suite.

Designing Woman

Siobhan grew up on a farm in a two-hundred-year-old house, with creaky doors and floorboards. "It was a wonderful place," she says, "but like all old houses, the rooms were small and the closets were practically nonexistent."

Her mother had a gift for making the old house beautiful, and Siobhan shared her interest. Her first job in the field was organizing, designing and installing closets for a national company. A few years later, she accepted a position with a local building supply company and began designing kitchens. It was here that she honed the skills that prepared her for building her own house.

"We used to visit my in-laws in Naples, Florida, and we loved walking around the neighborhoods looking at houses. I was always drawn to the Southern low-country style houses, which were set on stilts and had really beautiful staircases, porches and columns. I guess you could say I developed a bit of a 'Gone With The Wind' fetish. So when I designed our house, columns, verandas and sweeping steps had to be part of the design."

At the front of the house, the main entry is reached by a long, dramatic

A long, unpaved drive extends almost a third of a mile along an old stone wall to reach the property.

for John and Siobhan's large extended family and many friends; doors to the second-level veranda nearly double the entertaining space in fine weather.

Looking for Land

Lots that are still available for building are dear and rare along the coast of Connecticut. Places near the picture-perfect shore towns are out of reach financially for most folk. The average buyer-builder usually looks north, where old farms have been broken up and subdivided for residential development. But even though she and her husband did not meet the deep-pockets profile, Siobhan knew what she really wanted.

"I wanted a place near town, convenient to the highway and shopping, but secluded enough to give us a pretty landscape," says Siobhan. Her real estate friend told her about a large piece of land, just half a mile from the center of town, that was owned by a man who lived in a small house near the property's edge.

Researching the parcel, Siobhan discovered that the land had been used as a gravel pit for the town decades ago. There were significant wetlands on which nothing could be built. But there were three buildable acres. So the next task was to convince the owner to sell to her family.

stairway, and Siobhan specified round columns for the front-porch construction. The first level of the house includes the garage and a walk-out basement. Facing the backyard, the house has broad verandas on both floors, also supported by columns. The result is graceful and slightly formal.

Remembering the creaky doors and sparse closets of her childhood home, Siobhan designed the public areas of the house with an open plan, reserving doors for the home's private spaces. She also made ample room for storage. The main room opens from a hallway that extends to each wing — master bedroom and bath on one end, home office and guest room on the other. The kitchen and great room provide an expansive gathering place

"He's a fellow who keeps to himself and lives quietly," says Siobhan. "He bought the property quite a few years ago, when land was much cheaper, and supports himself by repairing musical instruments – all the big rock stars have used him to maintain their guitars and such. Nobody really knew if he would sell a piece of his land to anyone, but my real estate friend encouraged me to write him a letter. So I did."

It must have been a very persuasive letter. After a bit of back-and-forth negotiations, the owner agreed to sell just the three buildable acres – at the price that Siobhan and her husband had agreed was their limit. "Everyone's still amazed when I tell the story," she says, "but back then, those three acres were a nearly impassable thicket of brush and second-growth woods. It was ours and it was situated where I wanted to be, but it was still a challenging piece of land to work with."

The Clearing

Preparing the site for building was a huge task. Siobhan had fortunately made many contacts with building professionals on the job, and this knowledge served her well, from start to finish.

"I had gotten to know a lot of experienced contractors through my design work, and because I was going to be my own GC (see box on page 23), I tried to find as many old-timers as I could, to be my subs. These are the guys who've seen it all, and they can really be invaluable when you're learning as you go."

Site clearing was assigned to a gent known as Five Fingers. "That's not a mobster nickname or anything," smiles Siobhan, "but clearing is difficult and dangerous work. Five is the sum of the digits remaining on this guy's hands. But he was really good." She recalls standing in her flannel shirt, jeans and work boots early on the morning that the heavy

Because Siobhan's house sits in the middle of a large piece of land that is undevelopable – except for her three acres – she has beautiful views from every window.

equipment arrived, waving the huge earthmover back along a stone wall to the house site.

"It was pretty scary, directing something that big. But I earned the respect of those guys for taking it on. We got along very well."

Camping

Just as Siobhan and her subcontractors had started the building process in earnest, her family's condo sold – far sooner than they had expected—and the buyer needed to move in almost immediately.

"It was July and since this is a summer resort town, there wasn't a rental available anywhere, for any price. So, we borrowed my sister-in-law's trailer (the one she uses for traveling to horse shows) and moved it onto the property next to the building site. After a really thorough cleaning to get rid of the strong aroma of horse, we moved in. Of course, the building schedule suffered the usual glitches, like bad weather and other unforeseen work delays. We lived in the camper until late November."

Roughing it was a challenge. During the warm-weather months, while John was on vacation from his teaching job, barbecue and showers at friends' houses filled in some of the necessities. Once it got cold, and her husband was leaving early every morning for school, it got more complicated.

"My husband comes from a big family where hot, home-cooked evening meals are a tradition, and one that we've stuck to ourselves,"

Siobhan (standing) and her husband and daughter in front of their temporary "home."

says Siobhan. "Without a real kitchen, I had to improvise. I'd bring the ingredients for supper to work and cook them in the showroom's demonstration kitchen before going home. It might seem like a lot to go through, but we both appreciated those meals, especially on dreary, rainy nights when the camper was a lot less than cozy."

Basement living – crowded, but warm.

After almost five months, John and Siobhan were wrung out from their camping experience; the trailer was cold, and their daughter, Tara, was coming home from college for Thanksgiving. Just one week before the holiday, the new house was sufficiently enclosed and finished so that the family could move – this time, into the basement. "It wasn't great to live amid stacks of boxes and crates, but it beat the trailer by far!"

To the Ladder

Staying on schedule and on budget are the two major challenges of homebuilding, and Siobhan was determined not to live with any more chaos once the main floor of the house was finished.

"I wanted it *done*, to the last nail and the last can of paint." Because of time and money, John and Siobhan contributed many days of their own labor.

"When it came to siding our house, we decided to tackle it ourselves. We wanted to keep everything going, and we would have had to delay while waiting for a siding contractor.

I had to overcome my fear of ladders and learned to work fairly comfortably at the top of a twenty-footer, using both hands to place and nail the siding. I used the mantra 'Be the billy goat!' to get myself up that ladder every time."

Finish Work

All the little details that make a house look completed – molding along windows, ceilings and baseboards, built-ins, and surface coatings – are known as finish work. They require careful attention

Using the skills she developed while working on the house, Siobhan made a copy of an expensive antique table that she had admired. Her handmade repro cost just $150.

HERE'S A POINTER, FOR WOMEN ONLY

To store her hammer, a twelve-ounce model that she found most comfortable to use, Siobhan would hook it inside her brassiere when she was using her hands to fit the siding and place the nail. Also, she advises that those cute little gift bags with the string handles make excellent nail pockets. Just sling your belt through the handles. "I found it easier to use than a standard tool pouch," says Siobhan.

about getting along

As general contractor, Siobhan had to direct the work of many subcontractors, most of whom were far more experienced than she was. Here are some of her pointers on how to get the best results from subcontractors:

- One of the most important things I can share is that you should educate yourself. Try to learn something about every tradesperson involved in your project. Learn the basics of their language and they will respond much better to your questions.
- Avoid emotional reactions, no matter how much you want to have a tantrum. I've noticed that most of the men will shut down immediately if you lose it, and only remember what you did, not what you said.
- Follow up everything you discuss in writing, with an e-mail or fax. Work to be clear and concise in your requests. Never be afraid to ask questions. Engage your tradespeople in conversations about their craft; understand that this is what they do, every day of their work week.
- When there's a problem, and something needs to be fixed or changed, discuss it rationally, working to reach a mutually satisfying objective.
- Stay organized! Time is money for everyone.
- Think positively – keep the big picture in mind, and remember – there's nothing you can do about the weather!

to measurement and the smooth fit of all elements. Because this work is so labor-intensive, the cost for outside contractors can add up rapidly.

Siobhan's and John's friend, a contractor and talented finish carpenter, shared his expertise to help the couple install their own kitchen and all the molding throughout the house, as well as the trim for the house's eighteen columns. After subcontractors primed all the interior walls, Siobhan chose her palette and the couple painted everything themselves.

Rewards

Now that the house is completed — along with a pool and pool/guest house that Siobhan

Using a feature of Southern coastal architecture, Siobhan designed a double porch at the back of the house. It connects directly by stairs to the pool and guest house.

Siobhan has always loved lemon trees, and as a housewarming gift, a friend gave her a set of placemats with a lemon tree motif. "We'd been trying to decide how we would finish the backsplash around the stove," says Siobhan, "and when I saw those mats, I knew I'd found just the right thing. I called a tile artist the next day, and she hand-painted the backsplash tile. To me, it felt like just the right touch."

and John recently added — she has already set another goal for herself.

"The experience of building this house has given me the self-confidence I needed to take my work another step forward." In summer of 2004, Siobhan opened Cucina Design — her own kitchen design business. Her new showroom was only partially completed when clients started calling.

"It's so encouraging that I didn't have to wait for the phone to ring," says Siobhan. "I've been very busy since day one. And I'm so glad we built where we did. Home is only one highway exit away from the office."

"Every time I pull in the driveway, which is three-tenths of a mile long along an old stone wall, I am eager to turn the last corner where I can see the house and most of the yard. I get an enormous rush; such a huge sense of accomplishment, and so beautiful — it's a dream, come true."

THE GENERAL AND THE SUBS

Unless you can do all of the jobs involved in building a house — from clearing the land and preparing it for building, to hanging the last picture on the wall — you will need to hire many specialists, known as subcontractors or "subs," to complete each stage of the process — excavators, carpenters, plumbers, electricians, Sheetrock hangers, and so forth. If you decide to direct the building of your own house, you are the general contractor (the GC), chief of all subs. As GC, it is your responsibility to obtain the necessary permits; hire, schedule, direct, supervise, arrange for work inspection where needed and, finally, pay the subcontractors. It's a big and time-consuming job.

When you hire a GC, his (or her) remuneration is a percentage of the total bid for building. This means keeping materials, deliveries, and subs on schedule and on budget to make the anticipated profit. Inexperienced or unscrupulous general contractors who underbid actual costs may leave customers with a job that doesn't meet the original specifications or, worse, leave the job unfinished. If you want to be sure you've hired a good one, check references, talk with your prospective GC's customers, and visit more than one completed project.

Also be sure that your GC is a good fit with your personality. Because home-building involves literally hundreds of small decisions, your GC will be in as close contact with you as a family member, for many months. You should get along.

Alison Kennedy

A DREAM IN THE DESERT

"I love my house like a friend. I have a relationship with it, complete with ups and downs, good days and bad days, affection and regrets."

Alison applies grout to the kitchen's mosaic-tiled kickspaces.

ALISON KENNEDY never expected to become a homebuilder. It happened by default. After she and her boyfriend — a carpenter — had poured the footings of the house he had planned to build with her in southeastern Utah, their relationship hit the skids. He departed.

"I stared at that hole in the ground for six months," she says. "And then I decided to go for it, with absolutely no building experience. If there is a goddess of perseverance and determination, she was my guide."

The Design

"The decision to build the house myself came out of some inner desire to see if I could do it," says Alison. "But the design came from some creative place inside me that felt like the same place I used to tap as a little girl, when I drew pictures of houses, made interior design plans for my bedroom, rearranged all my furniture, or painted a picture in art class. It was a playful experience in a lot of ways — a big art project."

The house is framed with timber — interior beams were salvaged from an old one-room schoolhouse in a

space: 1,149 square feet • **best deal:** a $3,000+ roof for $100 (see p. 26) • **time to complete:** $5^1/_2$ years • **key accomplishments:** sculpted adobe animals in the walls; every one of the 900 sandbags that my friends and I filled to make the walls.

Alison's kitchen is softly illuminated by morning light, captured by an eastern window.

Left: An open plan gives the small house an expansive feel.

nearby community. To get the effect she wanted, Alison peeled the bark from locally harvested ponderosa pine logs, preferring their rustic texture to milled posts. True to southwest tradition, the walls are finished with adobe plaster, which covers the earth bags that create the walls around and between the structural wood skeleton.

"Sometimes I would think about things for a long time, going over and over something, without an apparent solution. Then, eventually, the answer would just present itself."

The walls go up: Alison's birthday parties turned into building parties, with many friends helping out. She fashioned a handmade tamper (right) to pack the earth-filled bags close together.

Knitting the Roof

Money was always tight over the five years Alison spent building the house. Putting on the roof — a costly proposition when done by others, and a dirty and somewhat scary do-it-yourself job — tested her ingenuity on several levels.

Her local public radio station has a weekly call-in program, Trading Post, which enables listeners to swap or give away things they no longer want or need. Realizing that most people have leftover shingles after a roofing job, Alison called in and asked for them.

To her surprise and delight, she got more than enough material for her project. The only dilemma posed by this good free stuff was an aesthetic

A sea turtle graces a bathroom wall, one of many sculpted images that Alison created as she plastered the earth bags with adobe.

one: how to create an attractive sheathing composed of shingles in 24 different colors.

An accomplished knitter who has clicked her needles through complex garments, Alison saw the rainbow palette of roofing asphalt as an interesting test of her pattern-making skills. She got out some graph paper and colored pencils, and set to work creating the roof layout, incorporating every hue and shade of shingle in the final design.

Installing the roof was a bigger challenge. Working nights at a local restaurant to pay the bills, she would get home in the wee hours, rising at five in the morning to nail up shingles before the heat of the southwestern summer became too overpowering (high temperatures also soften the asphalt, making shingles susceptible to burned-in footprints when the mercury soars).

In the construction business, roofing is often considered grunt work, assigned to the helper class — those with the least experience, as well as the youngest and sturdiest bodies. "It was exhausting," sighs Alison, remembering one of the toughest stretches of her building program, "but I finished the project with only nine shingles left over." Total cost: $100, for a roof that admirers compare to a Navajo rug.

The Kitchen

"I love sitting at the kitchen table with all the light coming in the windows."

Although small in dimensions and simply appointed, the luxury of Alison's kitchen is in its fine details. Working with local tradespeople and artisans, she achieved comfort, utility and beauty in a small footprint.

The graceful curve of the lower cabinets was accomplished with the help of a local carpenter, who steam-bent the alder wood doors for a distinctive, sweeping effect. Alison did most of the work on the concrete countertop herself, and used the forms for a swimming pool edge to create its broad, rounded profile. While all of the cabinet pulls hail from a nearby home center store, she hired a local metal artisan to fabricate complementary hardware to support the wall shelves and the narrow cottonwood bar counter that mounts above the main top; her small extravagances enhance the overall look of handcraft and elegance.

Almost all of the tiles in the house are salvaged, with the exception of hand-painted Mexican tile around the kitchen sink. For the kickboard underneath the cabinets, Alison pieced together bits of salvaged tile. On one of the days we spent talking and taking photographs, she finished one more project: grouting in her kickboard tile work.

Alison used broken pieces of salvaged tile to create mosaics on passageways between spaces (left). She cut other tiles to fill in the kick space beneath kitchen cabinets.

Reduce, Recycle, Reuse

Building a house with a small footprint was just one way that Alison tried to keep her project earth-friendly. Fallen timber from her land, such as the cottonwood logs used for the bar counter and part

South-facing windows with deep exterior overhangs provide passive solar efficiencies for the extreme desert climate.

of the cabinet framing, was free; a local sawyer milled the lumber on-site. "We didn't have to cut any live trees, because the low humidity of the desert prevents fallen wood from rotting. And there were no trucking costs for this lumber."

The thick walls of her house provide the mass necessary to keep the house surprisingly cool in summer, and warm in winter, which is no small accomplishment in the radical desert climate. A radiant under-floor system in the bathroom, plus a woodstove, supports the heating plan.

Alison reused salvaged materials, with mixed results. While the salvaged framing materials, glass block and tile enhance her home's aesthetics, she is less fond of the windows and doors that she had collected from the many places where she had lived before moving to Utah. "They are beautiful, and they were cheap, and they came from really cool places all over the country, but they leak like crazy and are a pain to operate."

Her advice to other women builders: invest money in high-quality, energy-efficient windows and doors — they are well worth the cost.

Stretching

Construction on a tiny budget has many drawbacks. Alison spent the first couple of years living in a camp trailer

Thick adobe walls provide rustic, tactile framing for the windows; Alison used salvaged glass block above the casements.

while she worked on the house. Then, when she hit a serious cash pinch, she sold the trailer to keep going and moved in, without a finished bedroom or kitchen. "Dust was everywhere, all the time," she remembers. "I had to wash the dishes in the bathtub."

In spite of her Spartan circumstances, Alison did find some benefit in occupying the unfinished house. "Living here helped me develop the space organically." As she worked and lived amid the dirt and clutter, she became aware of her own living patterns, which helped with the finishing details — and would not have been so obvious had she remained in the trailer. She felt the experience helped her make better decisions. And there were lots of those.

"When you're building, you have to make so many decisions, all the time, and it can be exhausting. So many people wanted to give me advice on how to do things — most of them men, many of them contractors and builders. It was a continual challenge to sort through their advice, figuring out which to follow and which to discard, and respecting their expertise yet retaining my vision for what I wanted my house to be."

Nowhere to run and short on cash, Alison lived in her unfinished house without a bedroom or kitchen.

Alison crafted all the copper wall sconces, which she installed on interior and exterior walls.

Below: Good free stuff: bright orange globe mallow — a flower native to southeastern Utah — has naturalized and spread around Alison's house.

"At times of stress, it was sometimes hard for me to tell whether my resistance to their ideas was just my stubbornness or my personal authority, and whether my acquiescence was humility, intelligent choice or lack of self-confidence. In the end, I made decisions from all those emotional places — some better, some worse.

"Just finishing the thing was a huge victory! I would say that the moment I felt the most victorious, the moment when it actually sunk in that I made this beautiful house, was when I stood back from the exterior paint job and admired the colors and designs as they dried in the sun. That really was quite a moment for me."

As any homeowner knows, a house is never *really finished.* Alison has her own wish list of improvements, which include big ideas, such as building an outdoor adobe fireplace and chimney, turning her little storage shed into an office and energizing it with a small solar panel, and finishing the landscaping.

"I love how open my house is. I love that it is simple, beautiful and unique. I feel so at peace in my house (when it is clean, anyway). It's a healing place to be. There is also a certain feeling that I get that it's hard to put a label on. But I guess if I had to name it, it would be 'pride.' Not a boastful, loud pride. It's a soft, quiet, peaceful pride, a true respect for myself and what I accomplished."

Alison's Do-It-Herself Achievement List

- ✔ creating house design
- ✔ filling and tamping the earth bags
- ✔ applying interior and exterior plaster and paints
- ✔ laying radiant heat tubing
- ✔ completing all mosaic tile work
- ✔ designing and shingling the roof
- ✔ building window boxes and frames
- ✔ building the mud floors
- ✔ making natural paint
- ✔ putting glass in doors
- ✔ laying glass bricks
- ✔ pouring, sanding, staining, sealing concrete countertops
- ✔ handling all landscaping
- ✔ designing and building the shed
- ✔ designing electrical plans
- ✔ installing all wiring, outlets, etc.
- ✔ installing bathroom wall covering
- ✔ mixing all adobe
- ✔ mixing and hand-pouring cement posts
- ✔ peeling log posts
- ✔ pouring and forming buttress footers by hand
- ✔ installing part of the tongue-and-groove ceiling
- ✔ installing lights and fans
- ✔ making all the copper sconces by hand

Tracy Ransom

WITH A LITTLE HELP FROM HER FRIENDS

"We love the porch and we sit out here in the morning with coffee, and in the evening to catch the breeze."

Tracy, hesitant at first, has overcome most of her fear of power tools.

ON A FROSTY SATURDAY morning in early April, you can see your breath in the chilly air. Up and down the block in Hartford, Connecticut, women are getting out of their cars, dressed in jeans and hooded sweatshirts. Some wear woolen caps; some are carrying toolboxes and bags. In singles and pairs, they begin to assemble around back of a two-story, gray-shingled house; this dwelling looks sharp and new, nestled between older, more worn-looking houses. Orange plastic netting around the perimeter and tall red ladders leaning against the front porch roof signal that work is going on here.

Building Blitz

A building blitz is about to begin — four days of finish work on a two-story house that's been constructed by the homeowner, Tracy Ransom, and a Women Build crew of dedicated volunteers. This long weekend is the culmination of six months of effort; after the details are finished, the house will be ready for its new family.

space: 1,248 square feet • **best deal:** overcoming my illness, and being chosen for the Women Build project • **time to complete:** 7 months • **key accomplishments:** being able to build the little details I wanted, becoming better organized to make the house beautiful inside, making wonderful friends while working on this project.

women
BUILD
GMAC
FINANCIAL
SERVICES

Habitat for Humanity is a world-renowned interfaith housing ministry that works with people in need to build simple, decent houses. A number of years ago, its founders and directors realized that half their volunteers were women – yet only 15 percent of these willing participants had any real experience with tools and building. Since 60 percent of Habitat homeowners are female heads of household, it was also critical that these women learn the physical skills required for home repairs and maintenance. The Women Build program grew out of a need to provide a safe and encouraging environment where women could feel comfortable learning and performing home construction. Since 1991, more than 450 Women Build homes have been completed by Habitat families and all- or mostly-female volunteer crews.

It's eight in the morning, and as the crew leader assembles small groups of women for the various work assignments, volunteers scatter to every corner of the house. Today's tasks include painting the basement, hallways, and second-floor bedrooms and bath; hanging closet doors; finishing woodwork on the stairways; and continuing work on the front and back porches.

The house is cold – its furnace has not yet been installed – so the main floor, drafty from

The volunteer painting crew hard at work.

movement in and out of the back door, is heated with a small propane unit, to help the paint dry. Everyone is dressed for wintry conditions; no one complains. With forty women at work in a small space, it is really very quiet. Walking around, one can hear the hum of power tools, the slap of a wet paintbrush against a wall, an occasional thump as women move doors around to attach hinges. Each woman focuses intently on her assigned job.

Many urban Habitat houses are designed with porches.

Below: Guys allowed—male volunteers are welcome to share their know-how.

Tracy is on the second floor, working on shelves in the bathroom. The tub enclosure has left a foot-wide, ceiling-high space between the tub and outside wall, and she is determined to fit some extra storage in this gap. "I need space for all my bathroom stuff," she smiles. Determination should be her middle name.

Living in a small apartment with two sons, Tracy had heard about the Habitat program several years before. She applied, but then life intervened. A diagnosis of cancer postponed her dreams of home ownership. She proceeded with treatment and, months later, emerged with a good prognosis: the cancer was in remission. In 2003, she was accepted as a Women Build homeowner.

A Habitat house is not a charitable gift to someone in need. Homeowners contribute hundreds of hours of their own labor as sweat equity in their houses. They need to come up with a down payment, and pay off their no-interest mortgage over time, just like any other homeowner. Money raised from donors for each project, roughly equal to the cost of the lot and materials, offsets the cost of the house for Habitat, so the organization can continue to acquire property and build more homes.

Work progresses and break time approaches. As the women relax into a rhythm with their work, happy chatter is added to the other sounds. The volunteers share stories, a team leader offers encouragement to a newcomer, and Tracy talks about colors and where she'll put things. Her house is starting to really look like . . . a home, in spite of the paint buckets, the sawhorse-workbench and the plastic tarp over the new carpet in the bedroom. Things are shaping up.

The women snack on sweet rolls and coffee. The buzz of conversation intensifies. I chat with volunteers.

"I went on the Internet, looking to volunteer my time. I wanted to help somebody and also help myself. The first time I showed up here, I was scared. I didn't know anything about building. Now I love it. I want to be part of the next project," says one woman.

Another says, "I'm exhausted when I go home but I feel great. This experience took the mystery out of homebuilding. It's so much fun, and it's really not that hard. Now I know why guys like to hang out in hardware stores."

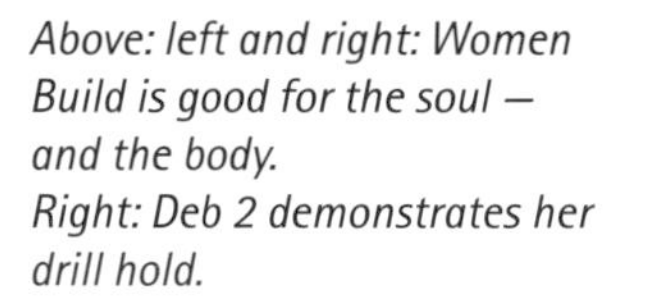

Above: left and right: Women Build is good for the soul — and the body.
Right: Deb 2 demonstrates her drill hold.

Shaping Up

While everyone enjoys the break, work resumes at the appointed time. Doors are moving into place. Two volunteers — they call themselves Deb 1 and Deb 2 — are hanging a closet door on

Porch rail, lattice, new shutters and Tracy's infant garden are the happy signs of a finished house.

the main floor. Deb 2 sports exquisite red fingernails, and has perfected her drill hold to preserve the manicure. "See?" she says as she screws the hinge into place, "Not even a nick."

The volunteers are a diverse bunch: single women, marrieds with and without children, college students and retirees. Some hail from the Hartford suburbs, with volunteers coming from as far as fifty miles away. Other women are city dwellers; one or two are prospective Habitat homeowners, preparing for their own building projects by helping with this one. The common denominator here is a willingness to learn and to help someone else. This spirit makes the building site feel like one big, joyful prayer.

Outside, finishing touches are made to the front porch roof. Although Habitat's rules specify simple house designs with modest appointments, homes in urban areas qualify for a front porch. Kathy Dolan, who manages the Women Build program for the Hartford chapter, explains. "The urban lots that Habitat buys are usually in run-down areas, because the land is less expensive. We've found that a front porch gives a Habitat house real presence in its neighborhood. Our Habitat families use their porches, and this discourages troublesome characters from hanging around."

Upstairs, two women are trying to ease a door into its frame; it doesn't quite fit.

One calls out, "I need a . . . you know . . . what's that thing you use to shave wood?"

"A plane," someone answers from the next room, "I'll get it."

The collaborative environment encourages an easy give-and-take. The women work all day, breaking for lunch but otherwise committed to complete their jobs.

"My reward is seeing all the progress we make by the end of the day," says one volunteer. "Sometimes the work is really slow stuff," she adds, "especially when there's a lot of measuring, cutting and fitting. But what we did today, it makes the place look really nice."

Dedication

On Sunday morning in late April, the weather has turned balmy. The paint is dry, the orange netting has been removed and Tracy's house is now in move-in condition. To celebrate the completion of Hartford's second Women Build project, volunteers, major sponsors, neighbors, friends and family have gathered to mark the occasion with prayers, thanks, house tours and refreshments. Tracy is beaming as she accepts a tool kit and a Bible, move-in gifts from the Hartford Habitat chapter. Volunteers bring little presents – plants, linens and framed photographs for the walls. One volunteer tells about

Left: *Tracy celebrates with friends from the Habitat crew. "We call ourselves the Power Girls."*
Far left: Tracy shows off shelves she designed and built.

another who took Tracy shopping at a home center store shortly before the dedication.

"She wanted to help Tracy keep her new kitchen in shape. Habitat's budget does not allow for things like kitchen hardware, but Tracy has teenage boys who probably won't pay much attention to the fingerprints and food that get on cabinets when there aren't any knobs. The volunteer told Tracy to pick out knobs and gave them to her as a housewarming gift. We're all just so excited to see Tracy have her dream.

"By the time we finish a project, we are friends. And a bunch of us like to maintain our friendships with Habitat families."

Housewarming

"This is my first real party," says Tracy, as we walk into her backyard on a warm, sunny August afternoon. She has been planning the celebration for a month. Chicken and frankfurters cook on the grill, homemade salads stay cool under foil covers, sodas chill in covered tubs. Tracy's friends and family – a cluster of Habitat volunteers among them – sit chatting at tables that have been set up around the yard. Music from a portable player surrounds us as Tracy makes introductions all around. Her joy is infectious; smiles are everywhere.

"When we lived in the apartment, there was never any room to entertain," she recalls, "so I've been dreaming about the day when I could share my happiness with everyone."

As the afternoon progresses, Tracy invites clusters of friends in for a tour of the house.

"I'm trying to organize as I go, and keep everything very neat and uncluttered," she says.

She proudly displays the shelves she had lobbied for, and built, in the upstairs bath.

Out front, shutters grace the windows, and Tracy has started landscaping with a few small plants and shrubs.

Home at last: Tracy and her son, Nathan, enjoy the front porch.

"We love the porch," she nods, "and we sit out here in the morning with coffee and in the evening to catch the breeze."

Lizabeth Moniz

VERMONT TWO-STEP

"I knew by the time I was a teenager that I wanted to build my own house. So I started moving toward that goal by learning how."

Lizabeth recalls the origins of her dream of a home of her own.

FROM CHILDHOOD, LIZABETH always enjoyed working with her hands. "I was fascinated with how things fit together," she says, "and I knew by the time I was a teenager that I wanted to build my own house. So I started moving toward that goal by learning how."

She enrolled in the first girls' shop class ever taught at her high school in Fairfax County, Virginia. "I had to fight to get in," she remembers, "and just the fact that they had a boys' class and a girls' class tells you something. The guys had the killer tools; we had the rejects." But she was not deterred.

After high school, she went to college looking to major in woodworking for a fine arts degree; she finished with a concentration in pottery. Out in the real world, she enrolled in an apprenticeship program so that she could start work as a carpenter. At the time – twenty-three years ago – she was the only woman on any of the crews she worked with. "It was kind of tough in those days," she recalls. "Being the new guy on the job – and a female – was challenging."

space: 1,840 square feet • **time to complete:** 2 years • **best deal:** bought windows at a spring truckload sale, saved 60 percent—thousands of dollars! • **key accomplishments:** cutting the timber frame; making all of the tiles for the shower; keeping our relationship together throughout.

The path from the driveway leads to the sun porch entry; its large windows provide beautiful views of the surrounding woods.

Fast forward a couple of decades. We meet Lizabeth outside the timber-frame house that she and Skip Dewhirst, her partner and husband for the last decade, have built on a big piece of land in rural Vermont. Woods and fields surround the house, and on this morning, a soft mist gives the landscape an almost magical quality. Bat, Skip and Lizabeth's black housecat, poses charmingly by the shop entrance to the house.

We walk up the path to the main entry, to see how Lizabeth's teenaged promise to herself has turned out.

hand-crafted. We wanted a place that expressed who we are."

Who they are is inextricably linked with forest and trees. Lizabeth's career in carpentry has continued, even though working in a very male environment was daunting at first. She now teaches the women's carpentry course at Yestermorrow school; with Skip, she teaches an annual design/build class in Costa Rica – scheduled in midwinter, when both need a break from the frigid Vermont climate. Her husband is a gifted woodworker who teaches timber framing and a wide variety of shop skills at Yestermorrow. He also builds beautiful custom furniture and fine musical instruments. Know them a little, and you would have no doubt that a house of wood was destiny.

Skip works on a special project – a spoon to be given to friends for an anniversary.

The Design

"We didn't want to buy someone else's prepackaged dream. Of course, you have to work within the constraints of money and the lay of the land. We did a lot of work before we got to the building stage, looking at other houses that were

The First Step

After they found their land, Lizabeth and Skip approached their dream house in a logical sequence. First they needed a base of operations. They designed a tiny cabin, set far back on the

Lizabeth nicknamed the first house the Makita Cabin because its turquoise trim matches the toolmaker's signature color.

property, with very modest amenities. They began building it in May, and by October they moved in.

Without running water or electricity, the cabin is warmed by a woodstove, serviced by an outside well-water pump, and there's a backhouse (outhouse) down the path. "We were young and full of dreams, and living there was an adventure of sorts," says Lizabeth. Having served in the Peace Corps in Lesotho (a tiny country completely surrounded by South Africa), the pair was conditioned to minimalist living. They spent the next two-and-a-half years in the tiny dwelling.

Step Two

With temporary living quarters taken care of, Lizabeth and Skip could focus on the shape their main house would take. They visualized a timber frame that emerges from a gentle slope on the property; its entrance to the kitchen is accessed through a porch on the second floor, and a walk-out entrance from the first-floor shop is backed by basement utility space. Upstairs on the third level, they placed a large, open room that would serve as the master suite.

Framing It

Lizabeth and Skip love the tradition of timber frame; they wanted to duplicate the generations-old practice of raising the frame by hand, using a volunteer force of friends and family.

"A lot of timber-frame companies use cranes to lift the frame into place; we wanted to find one that would let us work with them on the frame, and raise it ourselves, the old-fashioned way," says Skip. They found the right framer, and got their wish.

"Everyone showed up for the framing," says Lizabeth, "Skip's family, lots of friends and my family surprised me by appearing unannounced. About fifty people took part in the enterprise."

"In Vermont, many folks build their own houses, so we have work parties. Everyone helps each

Framing memories: (left) pulling up the frame with a great tug and many hands; (center) Lizabeth sitting astride the second level, Japanese saw in hand; (right) the topping ceremony. When the frame is complete and the roof's ridgepole is set, tradition holds that the builder attaches a small evergreen to the peak. Although the origin of this practice has been lost, many carpenters think it goes back to the days of the Druids, an ancient tribe who believed in the sacred spirits of trees. Skip and Lizabeth stand below the evergreen.

other. Our friends would work right along with us, not only on the frame, but all kinds of jobs: pounding nails, painting walls, even digging the hole for the outhouse at our cabin."

After the frame was in place, the pair spent a couple of weeks sanding and oiling it.

The frame's knee braces, and much of the home's interior trim, were made with lumber cut from Skip and Lizabeth's land and milled on-site with a portable sawmill. They have strong feelings about using materials in a sustainable way. "Nothing is more local than wood from your own land. It was a great way to use trees that we had to clear for the home site," declares Lizabeth.

Energy-Wise Heating

While the couple has a small, oil-fired furnace as a backup, most of the home's heat comes from a central chimney that provides warmth with a wood-fired masonry heater. Once the fire is lit in the main burn chamber, heat moves through a series of cavities inside the solid masonry chimney, warming the stack and the home's interior with radiant heat. This system burns wood so completely that almost no residue remains once the wood is consumed, and even on the coldest winter days, the fire needs to be stoked only twice: in the morning and before bedtime.

Central Vermont winters are frigid, but masonry

heaters are actually an old technology, used for centuries in the northern reaches of Europe. Clean burning and fuel-efficient, the system has kept the house warm through the coldest winters with just a cord-and-a-half of wood.

Lizabeth appreciates the heater's efficiency, but since it is a central feature of the open-plan house, she wanted it to be beautiful as well. Always careful with expenditures, Lizabeth haunted a nearby stone supplier, drawn to a local variety of stone that she thought would make a perfect facing for the chimney. "I went there looking so many times that the stone yard manager finally gave me a price," Lizabeth smiles. She loves a bargain, and has the perseverance to obtain one.

Mistress of Materials

"When you're on a tight budget – and we always have been – shopping carefully is a given. And there are good buys to be found. All you need is the time to find them and a place to store the stuff!"

In addition to the cabin, which Skip and Lizabeth still rent to tenants

One of the aesthetic pluses of a timber frame is its beautiful geometry. Lizabeth also uses some of the frames as shelves for her treasures, such as the baskets (opposite, top) that she collected during her Peace Corps assignment in Africa.

Skip and Lizabeth's masonry heating system offers a fire-viewing glass door and mantel on the living room side. A working bake oven faces the kitchen, left.

who don't mind roughing it, Skip also built an enclosure for materials not far from the house and shop.

This provides a place for the raw materials for the couple's work — dimensional lumber and hardwood for woodworking projects — as well as material that will eventually find its way into their home's finish details.

Lizabeth, with her training in pottery, has produced hundreds of handmade, hand-glazed tiles that will eventually be used in the house. In a three-quarter mudroom bath on the main floor, the tiles will decorate the wall of a shower enclosure. Also in the shed are boxes of smooth river rocks that Skip has collected over many summers of whitewater rafting trips that he has led in the New England wilderness; they will become the floor of the shower, "when we finally get to it," says Lizabeth.

But many other things have already found a home. One of the kitchen counters was a remnant piece of granite; a work surface next to the stove was the sink cutout for the long kitchen

The storage shed was built a few paces from the shop door; it shelters wood-working supplies, and materials destined for remaining projects in the house. Above, left, Lizabeth's prized $50 window; right, view toward the porch entry.

counter. "We already paid for it when we bought the solid surfacing for the kitchen — this is a great way not to waste it."

Along the back of the house, which still awaits some finishing, is a glass block bulls-eye window; it is installed in the shower enclosure. This type of glasswork is beautiful, and usually expensive. But Lizabeth found a way to fit the lovely detail into her budget.

"I saw that window in a bath-supply showroom a few years ago; it was part of a display, and I really wanted it. I made friends with the store manager and told him that I loved it but could never afford it. Later, when the showroom was changing displays, the manager told me that if I could get it out of the display, I could have it for $50. That was all the encouragement I needed. I came back with my reciprocating saw, cut it out and brought it home in my truck . . . a great score!"

Hurdles

"We did everything but pour the foundation, install most of the plumbing and tape the Sheetrock. We also hired a crew to help us put up the siding, as we knew it would take us forever.

Keeping our marriage together was the biggest challenge. So many decisions, and so much stress,

Except for the solid surfacing on the cabinet wall, all kitchen counters were fabricated from inexpensive remnants of otherwise pricey material. Lizabeth found and stored the materials until the couple was ready to finish the kitchen.

money pressure and the like don't make for a carefree relationship. You know the saying, 'Build a house, lose a spouse.' I can easily see the potential. But we made it."

The Future

Now that her own house projects are winding down, Lizabeth has set her sights on another career. She recently received a degree in landscape design and looks forward to working on other peoples' gardens, as well as her own. "Landscape work puts a lot less stress on the body than carpentry does," she admits. And it puts her more closely in touch with the earth.

"I love all the wood in our house, and that you can see that it was made of trees. Too much of new construction covers everything with Sheetrock and paint. I love our privacy from the road and from the neighbors. We live in the woods and I feel connected to the natural world in that way. We are surrounded by nature — that was one of our main goals. We have our private paradise in the woods."

Mary Kraus and Her Neighbors

BUILDING A COMMUNITY

"In celebration and in crisis, this community comes through."
—Flo Stern, PVCC member

Mary examines a pear tree, part of an orchard planted by residents in community open space.

ALTHOUGH MANY PEOPLE WHO WANT to design and build their own houses associate the process with a rural piece of land, others do not feel so comfortable with the relative isolation of this solution. To some women — singles with a long commute, heads of families with children to raise and educate, and seniors who may be concerned with accessibility and the limitations that come with aging — a little house in the big woods may not be an ideal choice.

On the flip side of the coin, a lot in a planned development or a unit in a condominium complex seems bland — a mass-produced village with a cookie-cutter aspect and little of the social interaction that many households long for.

Those who like the idea of a personalized structure in a community setting might be happily surprised by the cohousing concept — a neighborhood development based on the condominium model, planned by consensus of all its residents. To many who have chosen cohousing as a home design, it captures the best

space: 32 units, 600-1,000 square feet each • **best deal:** convincing the town of Amherst that cohousing would accomplish their goals, and securing the land • **time to complete:** 5 years • **key accomplishments:** a vital community; great cooperation, in spite of occasional struggles.

Left: Homeowners share the work and the produce from their community garden.
Top: A pedestrian walkway winds through the development. Space for cars is a short walk from the outside perimeter of the cluster of homes.
Bottom: Before sitting down for community suppers, members and guests gather for introductions, news, and a song.

of traditional, small-town America. Since cohousing communities attract populations where a majority of home-owners (about two-thirds) are single women or female-headed households, they are a particularly interesting choice to explore in this book.

The Beginnings

Amherst, Massachusetts, is a beautiful New England town, nestled among green hills and the fertile farms of the Connecticut River Valley. Home to Amherst College and a rapidly expanding state university, the town had a tract of 25 acres that it wanted to develop with a goal to create more affordable housing. It was here, after a false start with a conventional tract development, that Pioneer Valley Cohousing Community (PVCC) had its beginnings.

"My architectural firm was able to clear the affordable housing requirement of developing this land by allocating almost a third of the units — ten of thirty-two — for families that met the guidelines to qualify," says Mary Kraus of Kraus/Fitch Architects. "The rest of the units could be purchased at prevailing market values.

Top left: Thirty-two housing units are clustered, village-like, on five of the community's twenty-five acres. The common house can be seen in the right foreground.

Kitchens three ways: to keep the costs of units as low as possible, every kitchen was outfitted with lower cabinets; residents had the option of adding upper cabinets, shelves or other storage spaces at their own expense. On this page are three PVCC kitchens, all galley-style, done in three different configurations. Mary Kraus' kitchen (page 54) shows another way that residents customize according to their own needs and tastes.

It was a long process: to get clearance for the kind of development everyone wanted, to design houses that would be affordable and desirable, and to get the group to agree, or at least support, all the major decisions."

Developers are familiar with planning processes that take five or ten years, especially in desirable communities where current residents are often afflicted with a wary pessimism — usually born of experience — about new construction on a larger scale than a simple, single-

family dwelling. But a group of ordinary families interested only in housing themselves can find the long process of building a cohousing community daunting.

Coming to decisions that all participants can support, even when these decisions are not wholly satisfying to all, is a process that requires meetings and long discussions over many months. Like other cohousing communities, PVCC had its share of challenges. Gathering the requisite number of homeowners and then planning a community by consensus was a commitment that lasted five years from concept to move-in day.

A Personalized Community

What Pioneer Valley homeowners came up with was a cluster of farmhouse-style homes – some attached duplexes and triplexes, others freestanding single residences – laid out along a central pedestrian pathway. This left a considerable amount of open acreage for other uses. In addition, the homeowners agreed on a large common house that would contain a number of features that community members could use and maintain as a group. This centrally located common space gives every household, regardless of size, access to a professionally equipped community kitchen and dining room, laundry, sauna and shower, library, recreation area and play yard, as well as two guest rooms that homeowners can reserve for visiting friends and family. All these amenities are shared, allowing individual households to live within smaller and more affordable building footprints.

"Our priorities, which reflect shared values of the group, included child- and pedestrian-friendly home siting, economy of building size, energy-conserving building design and sustainably procured materials, and simplicity and cost-lowering efficiencies in finish details," says Mary Kraus, who was lead architect for the project and now lives with her husband in one of the small duplex units.

Mary's unit is typical of the smaller floor plan used in the design of PVCC: a galley kitchen and first-floor bath, a small open living area and an

Some features of Mary's house: a simple eat-in kitchen, the family piano, and John's workshop.

upstairs that could be finished as a loft space or enclosed as a large single bedroom or two smaller rooms. In Mary's duplex, two families share a single building envelope and a common porch. Mary's upstairs is a single enclosed bedroom, and her basement area is a workroom for her husband John's business — he makes violins and other stringed instruments.

Like most of the buildings at PVCC, Mary and John's place has a large south-facing roof area — ideal for utilizing solar power when a homeowner's budget permits. A few years ago, the couple installed solar panels to heat their hot water and save on electric bills.

Open Space

With homes, common house, jointly owned office and shop space using just six of the 25 acres, and an additional small area allocated to cars and pathways, PVCC has utilized the property's open landscape in a variety of ways that benefit the whole community.

There are community gardens, a fruit orchard and chicken house cared for by the residents, a common clothesline for those who want to dry their laundry the old-fashioned way, and fields and woods where homeowners, their families and guests can hike and enjoy the native flora and fauna that continue to thrive in this setting.

Walking around the community, one is struck by the quiet, punctuated on occasion by a group of children playing outside the common house, or by a passing flock of birds calling to each other as they fly overhead. Because cars are relegated to parking areas on the outer perimeters of the built space, vehicle noise is practically nonexistent. Tranquility reigns.

The Work of Community

Residents meet on a regular basis to consider how the various common efforts are working. Improvements are discussed and settled on by

Residents share chores, like collecting paper for town recycling, or serving at the community suppers.

consensus. And twice a week, on Mondays and Wednesdays, community members share an evening meal in the common house, cooked in its large, professionally equipped kitchen. These dinners are planned, prepared and served to all by small groups of residents who take turns with this task on a rotating basis. For many women, this regular respite from the responsibility for meal preparation is a wonderful perquisite of the cohousing experience.

Many residents also participate in a community food cooperative, saving money, time and gasoline through bulk buying, with all food delivered by the supplier to the common house.

For families, a closet-sized area in the common house called the "take it or leave it corner" is a great place to recycle outgrown clothing to other families in the community. Like the town square, the common house is a resource that brings the community together on a daily basis. Mail is delivered by the post office to its mailroom, play dates happen, kids study together and women chat or work together. Activities go on in a variety of gathering spaces available in the six-thousand-square-foot center. In the winter, a large fireplace becomes a cheery focal point for sharing conversation, board games or live musical performances.

"People attracted to cohousing have a need to create community," says Dyan Wiley, single parent and PVCC member since the first year of the planning stage. "This tendency to want to gather is very strong among women. Cohousing creates a great opportunity to come together, while maintaining a private space for each household that reflects its individuality. Like everyone else, I participated in the design of my own house. Pioneer Valley is not a commune — we are middle-class

Audrey Child's house: "I was lucky to be able to use the original design of a smaller unit, which included the loft. I didn't need the extra bedrooms and my workspace uses the loft. I'm happy to be clustered and semi-attached; I am at the stage of life when simple suits me perfectly." The kitchen/living space , above, is beautifully coordinated with dashes of bright turquoise. Audrey painted cabinets (left, background) in favorite hues.

families who value our personal space and independence. Yet cohousing enables many of us who have strong environmental consciousness to balance our individual need for a home with the very positive benefits of a community that values earth-friendliness and sustainability."

Women and Cohousing

Pioneer Valley Cohousing is not unique in its female-to-male adult ratio; like most other cohousing communities, about 60 percent of the resident homeowners are women. Although each has her personal reasons for choosing the community, a couple of themes emerge from dialogue with the residents.

Sylvia Kriebel, an educator who founded a Montessori school in nearby Northampton, joined PVCC at its inception and is now in her seventies. Her thousand-square-foot house is "more than I need now," but it is close to the common house, and she loves having people nearby and hearing children's voices as they play outside.

"I know many people my age who are facing the dilemma of leaving a house where they've lived for decades because there's no one nearby to help them. I am grateful to be in a situation where I'm not so isolated. Here, there are people to help when you need them. The diversity of households also means that you're not segregated with your own age group, which is one of the big drawbacks of senior communities."

Flo Stern, a retired union organizer who also joined PVCC at its beginning, lives with her partner and two adopted daughters (over the years, the couple has made room for a number of foster children as well) in a three-bedroom home. Right now the house feels too small — her daughters are teenagers — and some of the early design choices have not worked to the total

Right and opposite: With cars relegated to community lots, kid- and earth-friendly transport share the paths.

satisfaction of early residents, who now have accessibility problems as they age.

"The community was built on a sloping site, and since I've had surgeries, getting up and down the path is especially difficult. But my neighbors have been wonderful — the community built a ramp for me in a day, and bought a golf cart for me and others who need it to get around. Originally, I thought there would be tighter friendships among residents. While this has not proved out, PVCC does act as a community — when there's something to celebrate, or when there's a crisis. And this is important to me."

Flo Stern and Mary Kraus both acknowledged that such contingencies as the infirmities that go with aging were not top of mind when the project was first developed. The community is now investigating building a few accessible housing units to address the needs of older residents. Mary, who continues to design cohousing projects with her business partner and fellow architect, Laura Fitch, notes that recent projects have been more sensitive to a community's possible future needs. "We chose more level home siting for Pathways Cohousing, which was completed in Northampton (about ten miles from PVCC) in 2000."

Women with young children find cohousing to be particularly family friendly. There are neighbors for their kids to play with, a safe environment without cars, places to explore and bike without leaving the community. And mothers easily swap babysitting hours, or find resident teenagers or seniors willing to help. One young mother noted that the guest room in the common house was a convenient retreat after a number of sleepless nights with her newborn. "My husband took over, and I was able to get a good night's rest just a stone's throw from home."

In the end, a cohousing community boasts the benefits and shares the drawbacks of any small village. There's the neighborliness and mutual support of a community where homes sit close by one another, and then there are the frictions that such proximity engenders. On balance, the positive seems to win the day. In ten years, less than a handful of households have moved elsewhere.

Patti Garbeck

INTO THE WOODS

"I started working with tools when I was twelve, so it was kind of a natural leap into carpentry when I left home."

Patti (at right) shows her carpentry students a model of basic framing layout.

"WHEN I WAS A KID, *I used to love to fix things. My mom worked, my brothers were into sports and I really liked tinkering around. My mother encouraged me—it was help around the house for her. I started working with tools when I was twelve, so it was kind of a natural leap into carpentry when I left home."*

One look at Patti's snug little house in rural Vermont, and you know that she is a woman with a taste for simplicity and a love of nature. Even though she owns a large piece of land, when it came to the construction of her own home, she preferred to follow the mantra "small is beautiful."

Though she has worked for many years as a carpenter, her first personal experience with homebuilding was to put up a small cabin on land that she and a partner bought in the early 1980s. That house came together over several years, literally week by week. "We'd take money left over from buying groceries and take it to the sawyer to buy lumber," she recalls. It was a rugged construction; the first year, she crafted the cabin's only windows

space: 1,000 square feet • **best deal:** tower bedroom — wonderful view • **time to complete:** 6 months to move in, 11-plus years to finish • **key accomplishments:** screened porch for summer living, a small footprint that works — most of the time; no mortgage!

A rear view of the house shows the stages of construction: first, the house and shed; then the screened porch; finally, a sun deck for the third-floor tower.

by recycling doors from cast-off florists' refrigerators. Improvements beyond bare necessities came slowly.

"It was years before the place had running water and electricity," she recalls. "But actually, living without modern conveniences has really helped me to be disciplined about using resources today. Even now, I've never had an electric bill over $12 a month."

When she and her partner split up, she decided to build a new place on her own — a natural conclusion for a carpenter-by-trade. She sold her ex-partner her share of the original property. "Fortunately, the land value had just about doubled, so I was able to buy another piece on my own."

The forty-eight-acre parcel was situated off a fourth-class state road in a sparsely populated section of rural Vermont, known for its sugar maple trees and dotted with small, pristine ponds.

"When I bought the land, it was being used by hunters and squatters. To get the project started, I thought I'd put up a shed for storing materials. I had some lumber delivered to the property in the fall, but it was promptly ripped off. That was not exactly the welcome to the neighborhood I had hoped for."

Undaunted, Patti moved up to the land in a small trailer, breaking ground for the house in the spring.

"When I think about it now, it was a bit scary, living in a camper so far off the beaten path, all by myself. I was raised in the suburbs, with lots of people around. Looking back, I'm kind of amazed that I did it."

Welcome: Patti's front entry, with shop door (left) and porch.

Bottom right: Patti's winter work suit hangs on the back of the entry. "That suit keeps me warm when I'm working outside in the middle of February. The little lace doily is for fun. My aunt gave me a bunch of them, so I've put them around the house in unexpected places."

Bottom, left and center: waney siding and hand made hinge for the shop door.

Inspiration

"I moved to Vermont at the tail end of the back-to-the-land movement, so it was always my intention to live lightly and in harmony with nature. I also wanted to live without the burden of a mortgage. So I tried to keep the building footprint simple and small."

Approaching her house from the driveway, the first thing you see is the beautifully crafted door to Patti's shop, made of boards laid diagonally, with a smooth finish and graceful wrought-iron hinges. The house is sided with waney wood clapboard; this is wood that has

not been planed to a straight edge, and has only the tree's bark removed. The tree trunk's natural curve becomes a part of the sheathing, creating an effect that is rustic, yet somehow quite delicate.

"The boards are sawn one-half inch thick, rather than the standard three-quarters," says Patti. "It makes the siding look smoother and more subtle than a finish with thicker boards."

So many of the home's surfaces reveal Patti's craft. It is reflected in the sturdy posts and beams, the artful trim around doors, the wainscoting and wide plank floors. This is a carpenter's house, where wood is queen.

The place is small — just a thousand square feet of living space. The first floor has a sitting/living area, a diminutive kitchen and a dining alcove. Upstairs is a multipurpose room — it functions as workroom, library and guest room when needed — a bath and a small hallway with a steep ladder-stair leading to Patti's third-level tower bedroom. With just enough space for a bed and a few

pieces of furniture, the bedroom offers beautiful views of the surrounding mountains. In all seasons, the vistas more than compensate for the cozy floor plan.

Construction

"Breaking ground was a big challenge. Seeing that huge earth-moving machine and the damage it could do, it didn't seem so low-impact. And of course, breaking ground in early May when the blackflies were at their worst made me question my choice of location."

Once the site was ready and the foundation poured, Patti did most of the work herself.

She paid a few carpenter friends to help her with the framing and to get the house under cover, and also bartered her carpentry skills with other tradesmen in exchange for the labor she needed. She hired subcontractors for the electrical and plumbing work, and then did all the finish work herself.

PATTI'S TIMELINE

1993: Moved in on Thanksgiving; painted Sheetrock, finished floor, no finish trim, 2- by 4-foot kitchen counters and bath vanity.

1996: Added on screened porch and third-floor deck.

1999: Sold solar electric system and hooked up to grid. Sad to change, but the solar was too expensive to maintain. Batteries needed updating, inverter had been hit by lightning, generator had to be rebuilt. All those years without electricity have paid off — no bill over $12 yet!

2001: Dirt floor woodshed begins to change to a shop, with floors and walls.

2002: Finally set Sheetrock and trimmed third floor.

2004: Shop is transforming into music room. Entrance will now be from mudroom; outside doors soon to become a big window.

Worth the climb: Patti's eighty-square-foot tower bedroom is a private, secluded retreat. Its deck provides a wonderful spot for sunning on a summer day.

She was also beneficiary of an unexpected blessing. Needing a chimney for the woodstove that heats the house, Patti hired her college roommate's husband.

"The whole family drove for ten hours to get here, then camped for four days while he built a beautiful brick-faced chimney. When I went to pay him, he refused to take any money and told me, 'That's what friends are for.'"

Moving In

Vermont weather can be unforgiving; spring arrives late, and winter is early where Patti lives. But in spite of having to work for a living while she worked on her house, she was out of the camper and tucked in on Thanksgiving Day. Discipline, an uncomplicated plan, and some long and tiring days made the result possible.

"It was a big victory to be able to move into my house six months after I began work. It's also great to have done it and have no mortgage. I owe thanks to my mother for leaving me some money to get the project started, and also for encouraging my interest in home repairs when I was very young."

Second Thoughts

Although Patti continues to work on her home's finish details, and is planning a small addition that will give her a bigger kitchen and more room for entertaining, she reflects on the initial process and what she might have done differently.

"Personally, I would have spent more time on the design. In such a small space, it's important to

use the square footage efficiently. It would have been nice to spend a year working on the land and get more acquainted with it before breaking ground, instead of moving so quickly to build. A slower pace would have enabled me to really think about the floor plan," she says.

"I also wanted to buy lumber from a local sawyer, which meant that the wood I used was still green. So unfortunately the diagonal sheathing (over the frame, under the waney clapboard) shrunk up. It left nice little entrances for all the field mice to move in! As a carpenter, I was aware that wood shrinks as it dries. Building my own house, I was definitely in a hurry. That's one more reason to take your time."

"Attention to detail saves a lot of work later. I wish I had taken more care in the beginning, preserving the wood and buttoning up the exterior. And of course, that I'd listened to everyone who told me, 'Don't move in until the house is all done.' At eleven years and counting, I still have things I'd like to do, but motivation wanes as time passes."

Simple Pleasures

As one would expect of a carpenter — a trade that requires

Patti's living and dining areas. A friend's husband built the chimney, and furnishings are simple. "Whatever I haven't built myself are gifts from friends." Below left, her garden is taking shape.

working outdoors in all kinds of weather — Patti enjoys her country haven. Skiing, hiking, canoeing and other outdoor pastimes are close to home. Her house is a quick ride from the radio station where she jockeys a weekly music program, although it's a longer trek to Yestermorrow Design/Build school, where she regularly teaches carpentry, woodworking and power tool basics to students from around the country. Her current project — before tackling the addition — is morphing her shop into a music

patti's advice

Patti has some practical guidance for other women who are planning houses, want to do a lot of the work themselves, and have limited resources.

- Don't bite off more than you can chew. It's easy to get overwhelmed.

- Start small with the possibilities of adding on. Frame up the shell and only live in a small finished area. I've known folks who have lived in the basement for a few years before building. Or, build a garage with an apartment above, to live in while you build the house. But do not move into the house until it's all done.

- Visit as many owner-built houses as you can. Talk to the owners and find out what they would have done differently. Learn from their mistakes.

- If you will be doing much of the labor and are not used to doing hard physical work, start doing yoga *now*.

While the formal entrance to the house is through the front door by way of a step-up, Patti loves her screened porch and has given some distinction to its entryway with a custom molding treatment.

Patti faux-painted her plywood kitchen counter to look like ceramic tile.

room; she is an accomplished guitarist as well as a deejay. Talking about her house, she sees it as a base and enjoys its connection to the world outside.

"I most love the wraparound screened porch. I live, eat and sleep out here in the warmer months. On this early spring morning as I write about my house, the sun is streaming in, the birds are happily singing, the gardens are in view and the bugs are outside! I love that I have no mortgage, and sometimes, when the house is feeling too small, I remind myself that I'm in Vermont. The land is beautiful here, and who wants to be indoors, anyway?"

Patti plans to expand the living area where the windows behind the couch are now. She also wants to improve the kitchen. But the refrigerator stays. It's actually a decommissioned, vintage appliance where she stores pots and pans.

Lisa Hawkins

RESOURCEFUL RANCH

"When I see the house at the end of the day, that magical time right after sunset, when snow is lying on the ground and the lights shine out, it looks sturdy and sheltering. It lies low on the slope, not overpowering the site."

Lisa applies plaster to strawbale walls.

"I'VE ALWAYS BEEN INTERESTED *in living spaces, and what makes me feel comfortable, uncomfortable, secure, or insecure. We moved many times when I was a child, because my father did not want to commit to owning a house. Some of these rented houses were furnished, and others were filled with our own things. So I was exposed to a variety of spaces and room arrangements, and probably registered what felt right and what jarred. I also liked to make little shelters in the woods, inspired by some books in the school library. When my parents finally bought a house, they had it remodeled by an architect, who did not do a very good job of it. I learned something from that, too."*

After she left home and married, Lisa continued to nurture her lifelong affinity for making spaces of her own design. She and her husband renovated one home. "We made the mistake of putting more into it than we needed to, and barely broke even when we sold it," she remembers. Lisa later owned two more

space: 1,144 square feet • **time to complete:** 16 months • **best deal:** finding the pool contractor for the clay sheathing — he saved me weeks of work • **key accomplishments:** a design I love, the home's great light and quiet; experimenting with technologies that really work.

houses in the Washington, D.C., area, renovating the kitchen in one, and transforming an attic into bedroom, bath and playroom in another. Both times, she made a handy profit.

When her four children were grown, Lisa left Washington for Vermont. She decided it was time to move into something she had designed herself. She read lots of books on passive solar construction, building with logs, how to wire, plumb, "and on and on," she smiles. Finding a job with a design/build company, she learned by osmosis how a house was put together. Then she took a course at Shelter Institute in Maine (see "Building Lessons," chapter 17). "That gave me the courage to sit down with graph paper and pencil and start thinking."

Her first house was a post-and-beam construction; she lived above the detached garage of this first house while the framer she had hired completed the main house. After enjoying this home for several years, she again felt the urge to move on. She settled in Maine to be closer to the ocean.

"The next house was a post and beam log home, and I learned the hard way that cedar logs alone are not sufficient insulation for Maine winters. Once the wall cavities were filled with blown-in cellulose, the place was much more comfortable.

"What led to this house, the one I live in now, was an invitation to join in a strawbale workshop construction in Nashua, New Hampshire. Why I got the notice is a mystery, unless it was because I was involved with a study group of building professionals and interested amateurs, who would get together to discuss energy efficient and healthy buildings.

By the time she designed her third house, Lisa knew how to insulate for cold climate. Her roof, with its handsome, broad profile, keeps out the cold with a thick layer of blown-in cellulose.

Thick strawbale walls create deep window surrounds and provide dramatic contrasts of light and shadow.

"I went to the workshop and met Matts Myhrman and Judy Knox, who have been guiding forces in the strawbale movement, I was hooked. Here was a building method that was beautiful and affordable. Now I wanted to build my own strawbale home!"

Inspiration

After the first workshop, Lisa enrolled in another natural building course in New Mexico, followed by several workshops led by Matts and Judy in Arizona.

"My father had been born in New Mexico, so it was exciting to go there. Some of us camped on the edge of the Gila Forest reserve and visited the cliff dwellings in the area. The builders of those cliff houses knew how to site them for the sun's warmth in winter and cool shadow in the summer. I helped build a strawbale guest house with a living roof (composed of plant material). So many interesting ideas, such organic structures! On one of the trips to Tucson, Matts and Judy invited me to stay in a small strawbale home built for Matts' mother. It was lovely—quiet, cool and something different about the feel of it. I felt more than ever that I had to build one."

A half wall surrounds the kitchen in Lisa's open floor plan. Entrance to office area is rear left, with loft in the gable above.

Lisa began searching for land near her Maine home where she could try her hand at strawbale, and found a parcel that she liked. That summer, she took another intensive design/build course and drew some rough plans.

"My site was good for a long, one story building running east-west. When using strawbales, it is easier to keep the walls low, and since I didn't know how much help I would have I kept it simple, with less to plaster."

The Design

The public spaces of Lisa's house are open to one another, with a ribs-high wall surrounding the kitchen area that has its work surfaces sheltered from view. The beautiful timber-frame roof structure is exposed from below; its sculptural dignity lends additional interest to the simple, rectangular space.

At the west end of the large main room, she

Lisa lived in a small guest house during the construction of the main house. She used the guest house as a trial run for learning strawbale building techniques before tackling the larger project.

has designed a step-up to an office area, with a loft above to be used as a guest sleeping area. Going east on the house's east-west axis, Lisa designed a hall to access the private spaces: a bath, master bedroom, spare bedroom/changing room and a small but well-thought-out utility room for managing all the house's systems. Windows at the east end, plus skylights on the roof admit morning light to the bedroom and bath. "It's wonderful to wake up with the sun," says Lisa.

Construction

To get a feel for working with strawbales, Lisa's first project was a small (20- by 20-foot) guest house with a shed roof. The structure was a personalized course in construction; straw is natural, renewable and inexpensive, but it has its own demands.

"I laid cinderblocks around the edge of the guest house slab, cementing them into place and then pouring vermiculite into the cavities for insulation. Rebar (long metal rods used to reinforce concrete) was cemented into some of the holes to pin the bottom courses of bales to the foundation. After that chore was done, I wrestled the bales between the posts of the frame.

"I devised a bale puller made from a piece of wood and a long piece of rope. First I'd put a bale into the end of

Top: Radiant floor tubing in place before the slab is poured.
Above : Baled-in frame of the main house.
Left: Contractor spraying plaster with gunite gun.

Wainscoting, doors, a half-height kitchen wall and the home's timber frame wear their natural finish. Lisa also used earth-friendly paints and stains throughout.

the wall, put the wood board behind it, and then go around and pull it into place with the rope. Jeff, my house framer, had not left any wriggle room, so sometimes I had to trim the edge of the bale to make it fit."

Once she finished the inside walls with tongue-and-groove pine and outfitted the guest house to be habitable, Lisa was ready to move in. It would be her home while she acted as general contractor for the main residence. "Finishing the outbuilding first enabled me to learn a lot of useful things, and I found that I could live comfortably in a four-hundred-square-foot house, heated only by a wood stove." After a few very cold winter nights there, Lisa augmented the stove's warmth with an old-timers' insulating trick—she banked the house with hay bales. "That took the chill out," she says, "and it helped keep the place cozy until spring arrived."

South-facing windows and a radiant floor heating system keep the house comfortable. The woodstove provides backup heat and supplemental warmth on the most frigid Maine nights.

The slab was poured in October, and Lisa worked side-by-side with the heating contractor and plumber to wire tubing for her radiant flooring system to the reinforcing mesh that floats above the insulation board. With friends, she covered the foundation with straw, leaves, tarps and logs to hold it down for the winter.

In the spring, the foundation contractor returned to form the rim around the slab, where the bale walls would rise. After Lisa applied sealant to the rim, she laid pressure-treated plywood along its surface; the bales would rest on this base.

When the bales arrived (Lisa bought them from a dealer in New Brunswick), she and a friend set the first course so that window and door frames could be installed. Then Lisa gathered a large group of friends to stack the bales in one big push.

"The group effort resulted in slightly crooked

The Main House

Lisa had rented a mechanical tamper while the guest house was going up, so that she could prepare the ground where the house slab would be poured; this step helps insure the integrity of the slab, preventing the ground from settling and doing damage later.

"I spent an afternoon with that machine, going round and round," Lisa remembers.

Lisa used simple pine sheathing for bathroom walls and a Japanese-style soaking tub. The room benefits from soft morning light.

walls, so I spent the next week tweaking bales and straightening the worst rows."

The next step was plastering. Lisa has a friend who spent days digging clay, breaking it down to a plaster and applying it to the walls of her house by hand. But knowing her own lack of patience with this tedious activity, Lisa went directly to the phone book.

"I found a pool contractor who used a gunite gun to make his pools. I drove to his office and asked if he would be willing to use his expertise to blow a mix of sand and clay onto some strawbale walls. He didn't fall down laughing, and when I told him I'd bring him a bale, some clay and sand, plus a check for renting a compressor, he said he'd experiment and let me know if he could do it. Yes! It was a go. Early one fall morning he came with his crew, and amid clouds of clay dust he blew the mixture onto the walls, with some of the crew coming along with trowels to smooth it down. At the end of a long, hard day it was done. It would have taken me weeks."

Lisa then whitewashed the walls with lime and filled all the worst cracks. She hired a plasterer,

who had moved back to Maine from New York, to finish the interior walls.

While he and a helper plastered, she finished painting. The house was ready to live in.

Enjoying the Process

As general contractor, Lisa was responsible for hiring her builder and all the subs for the installation of the systems and materials. Like many other owner/builders, she discovered that one good contractor could be the source of many others.

"I'm very grateful to Jeff Merry, my wonderfully kind and encouraging builder. He and his assistant, Tom Mackey, put up with this strange way of building. They were patient and willing to do other proj-

LISA'S GREEN HOUSE

The more Lisa's experience with home design and building deepened, the more thoroughly she committed herself to sustainable features and materials. In addition to strawbale, the new house incorporates other earth-friendly and energy-efficient features:

- Standing seam metal roof (will last 50 years); the roof is insulated with a thick layer (R-45) of blown-in cellulose, which accounts for the strong, deep roof profile.
- Passive solar design elements: south-facing windows and deep roof overhangs that keep the house cooler in summer, yet admit increased light in the cold winter months when the sun is low on the horizon.
- Grid-tied solar electric array (1 kilowatt) to provide sunpower and lower the cost of electric utility bills; a battery bank to run the solar power during outages keeps the refrigerator and some lights running. Lisa has a woodstove as backup for the hot water-heated–radiant floor system throughout the house.
- Highly-efficient on-demand hot water heating.
- Super energy-efficient refrigerator and laundry equipment.

For the past several years, Lisa has been director of the energy and shelter exhibits at Maine's Common Ground Fair — an annual gathering of farmers, businesses and artisans dedicated to sustainable living. Working on the fair has kept her aware of the latest developments in energy-saving practices and products.

ects while waiting for the bale walls to be built. Jeff knew the electrician, who became quite interested in my solar panel/grid intertie, so his recommendations were quite useful. Jeff had also worked with the tile setter, who did a beautiful job with my project. Because of Jeff, I was able to deal with local craftsmen, which I enjoyed far more than dealing with a big builder, who would have been more impersonal. Listening to their banter and sharing lunch time together put a good energy into the workplace, and that energy permeates the house to this day."

Satisfactions

"What I love about my home is the way the light moves through it. After several days of gloom and fog, the sky is clear and sunlight is pouring in. As the sun moves through its arc, it touches the kitchen through the skylights. Then, at the end of the day, the rich gold of sunset comes in through the western windows. It is quiet. Even if there is a howling snowstorm, I hear nothing and am surprised at how loud the wind is when I open the door. It is pleasantly cool on a hot day. I like the openness of the cathedral ceiling with its beams of pine, which are turning the color of honey.

"I am pleased with what I and my workmen friends have wrought."

Jill MacNaughton

THE HOUSE THAT JILL RENOVATED

"It's a great house for having people over — lots of people can cook together in my kitchen; I love that the kitchen and dining areas open to each other."

Jill at her entry-way window.

"I FIRST SAW THE HOUSE *in May, which means early spring in this part of Vermont," says Jill MacNaughton. "I was in love with it from the moment I drove into the little parking area by the side of the road. The birds were singing, and the light sifting through the trees was beautiful. It felt like the perfect spot. The house itself was unfinished inside, kind of a mess, really, but the location was gorgeous."*

Location, location, location. The mantra of generations of real estate agents makes perfect sense to anyone who's fallen hard for a beautiful piece of land with a not-so-spectacular house. *It's fine,* we say. *Look at that view. We can renovate.*

Jill MacNaughton wasn't really looking for a house when she first saw the rental property, its contemporary-style dwelling sitting uphill from the waterline of a pristine lake in central Vermont. But she so enjoyed her holiday there, surrounded by woods, water views and blissful quiet, that she knew what to do when she saw the "For Sale" sign leaning

space: 1,460 square feet • **best deal:** finding Patti Garbeck for the carpentry work • **time to complete:** 4 years • **key accomplishments:** a kitchen design that really works; organizing the project so I could use the house; keeping a sense of humor through four years.

The house and view to the lake, in early spring, when snow often lingers in the shady spots.

The Lake House: Year 1 (top left); Year 2 (top right); Year 3 (bottom left); Year 4 (bottom right). The timeline for a renovation expands in inverse proportion to available funds; in other words, the less money you have, the longer it will take. Because Jill's budget was limited, the interior construction of her house was completed over four years, in logical steps.

askew near the driveway as she pulled out. "I didn't notice it until then," she recalls.

She jotted down the phone number of the real estate agency, and then proceeded to buy the place, warts and all.

Inside the simple, 28- by 28-foot house, the previous owner hadn't made much progress. There were no interior doors, it still had its plywood subfloor, and Jill, who stands 6'1" in her bare feet, hit her head on the unfinished stairway leading to the bedroom upstairs. There was no inside staircase to the basement level; to access it, one had to walk around the outside of the house to a door at ground level. The kitchen had no counter space and no cabinets.

"But it had beautiful views to the lake," Jill smiles. Like all renovators, she is an optimist. Thus began an extended personal journey to make her new vacation house a home.

As an attorney working and living in a town some miles from the lake, Jill had the fortunate option of being able to get away from her getaway while major construction took place. However, she did not have the budget to get the process done in a short time. Instead, the space evolved over four years. This meant, among other ramifications, that she would have a close relationship with dust and debris for a very long time. Since she wanted to use the house during its transformation, she had to adjust to the mess.

Left: The staircase provides a partition between living and dining areas. A staircase to the basement now runs below it. Jill added the long window in the dining room to enhance her views from the kitchen.

Below: The living/entertaining area provides the most expansive lake views.

The Design

The interior of Jill's lake house now has a functional precision that reveals her love for order and simplicity. But the floor plan did not spring fully formed into her imagination. It was the product of six months spent looking at books and magazines, and sketching her ideas on graph paper. Many, many wastebaskets full of rejected plans went out with the trash before she had a design that she liked.

Even though she had no training as an architect or designer (she actually studied to be a teacher as an undergrad at McGill University), Jill had a heritage that gave her confidence to draw her own plans. Her mother had completely renovated the family home in Montreal when Jill was twelve years old. "My own kitchen is similar, though less formal

Jill chose wide plank flooring throughout the house. She stained and finished floors and woodwork herself.

than my mother's house," she says.

"Both my parents have built and designed several homes. They have great ability to visualize. Often, when I was trying to come up with a design solution, I'd call one or the other and describe my creative problem. They both were able to quickly 'see' and give great feedback over the phone."

Jill had to be very careful with the interior design. "For example, once you build a staircase, you don't want to do it again — stairs are difficult and expensive to move."

Working within the lake house's small footprint, she wanted to preserve (or amplify) her views, give the house at least an illusion of space and volume, and at the same time keep the plan simple enough for a limited budget.

She looked at lots of pictures in home design books and magazines, bookmarking ideas that she

In place of a plain wall and the old stair to the second floor (see page 82, year one photo), Jill designed open shelves and cabinets for kitchen storage. The shelves display raku *pottery made by Jill, her mother, and friends. She also made space to tuck in a stool, where she can sit while she chats on the phone or works at the counter. To left of kitchen shelves, Jill makes use of the passageway with a built-in bookcase behind the support beam.*

Drawers, not doors, flank the cooktop and built-in under-counter oven.

liked. She drew and re-drew the plans, creating multiple configurations for the rooms and built-ins until the design started to take shape.

"I'd advise anyone who wants to design a space themselves to have at least one technical book about measurement," she says. Knowing how buildings are put together, standard dimensions for lumber and framing — all these basics that an apprentice carpenter learns can also help the novice designer keep her plans grounded in the real world.

Once she had a pleasing design on paper, Jill would test out the concept, marking off the floor where counters and cabinets and stairwells would go. This thoroughness enabled her to check the design for things like traffic flow, head room and good vistas. When she felt clear about the design, she would fine-tune it with the detailing she wanted.

Year One

Before she bought the house, Jill consulted a local carpenter, Patti Garbeck (see "Into the Woods," chapter 6), who looked over the place before she inked the contract to buy it. "I am so grateful to have had Patti's help with this project," says Jill. "Like my parents, she has the talent to visualize things before they are in place."

Together, they worked out a plan for the renovation. The main floor had a step-down from the kitchen area to the living/dining space. "We raised the floor to a single level, which would make movement around the public spaces smooth and less hazardous," says Jill.

With Patti's carpentry skills, Jill also solved the staircase problem, using a single stairwell that runs from the basement to the second floor, and provides room for tall people like herself to negotiate between floors without ducking.

Finally, that first, expensive year provided Jill with an all-season getaway. She had a furnace installed. These three major improvements ate up her phase one budget.

Year Two

"Sometimes things have to get worse before they get better," says Jill. In the second year, the kitchen looked like more of a wreck than it was when she bought the place.

Jill wanted to make room for a home office space and shelves, a half-bath for guests on the main floor, and a laundry closet. To do this, she needed to frame in a wall in the area adjacent to the kitchen, where the old staircase had risen to the second floor. This partition would act as the back of the half-bath and laundry; the side facing the kitchen would be fitted with shelves and cabinets — but not yet.

Get a handle on it: pots and pans are easier to access with deep drawer storage.

"There was still no place to put anything, and using the kitchen was tricky," Jill remembers. Still, she made progress. Patti built a stair for the outside deck. "The fact that the inside wasn't finished was balanced by having a nice place to relax and enjoy the lake outside."

Anyone who does renovations begins to envy the lifestyle of plumbers; after the pipes were in place, year two's budget was fully consumed.

Year Three

The third phase of renovations revealed much of what the kitchen would eventually become. The wall of cabinets and shelves that back up to the half-bath/laundry closet wall were finished. Patti put the island in place; it stands taller than the standard 36-inch height to make a counter where Jill could eventually work and wash dishes comfortably.

"The kitchen was finally much easier to use," says Jill. Even though her full-time job left her little leeway for hands-on projects, she eventually became a painting expert; she has applied all of the coatings in the house, including finishing the wood stairs and wide-plank floors.

Year Four

With the end of major renovations in sight, it was time for finish work. In the kitchen, Patti installed a new window and countertops. After the appliances — a cooktop, under-counter oven, new refrigerator — and a new sink were in place, Patti finished off the cabinets. Instead of cavernous spaces behind doors, Jill had designed the

Sitting at her custom-built partner's desk, in the back corner of the main floor, Jill can look at her favorite view. "I spend so much time at the desk or at the sink that I made sure I could see the lake from both places."

under-counter areas around the oven and flanking the sink to accommodate deep drawers for storage. "Instead of bending and crawling around the cabinets to reach a pot or a bowl, I can store all of this equipment in easily accessible drawers. It really improves the efficiency of my small kitchen area."

Jill also used the recess between studs in the kitchen closet wall (adjacent to the cooktop counter) to make a built-in space for spices — a neat, economical storage solution, in just the right spot to serve its purpose.

The icing on the cake was a new outside stairway from the roadside driveway to the entry, which makes the steep incline safe to negotiate. It also adds a note of elegance to the simple shape of the house.

Second Thoughts

Now that her stint as a general contractor is just a memory, Jill reflects on the success of her design.

"It's true that you're always cleaning with a stretched-out renovation like mine. Living with sawdust for four years was a big challenge. But in the end, I was happy with the result."

Even today, the only glitch in her design is under the kitchen sink.

"If I did this again, I'd place the trash cabinet somewhere else; it always disturbs the person who's working at the sink!"

She would also like to be more hands-on. Patti gave her a small Japanese saw as a housewarming gift; she's used it to install closet and curtain poles, and cut drawer dividers. "It's such an elegant little tool and I love the way in cuts wood so easily. Even though I was working full-time, whenever I got the chance to watch Patti, it made me curious to try more things on my own."

Kathe Higgins

UP A MOUNTAIN

"I love my home. I love the location, the design, the windows, the high ceilings, the colors and the sense of serenity I feel when I walk through the door. My spirit soars."

Kathe loves working on the house, doing her own small repairs.

"EVER SINCE I WAS A YOUNG GIRL, *I wanted my own home, a safe haven, a sanctuary. I grew up in rural Massachusetts, in a small town about an hour north of Boston, where there were more dogs than people, and lots of green fields and woods. I would often escape to the woods because I felt safe there — no people, just critters and trees that reached to the heavens. This childhood experience gave me a vision for the kind of place where I would like to settle."*

Arriving at the foot of Kathe's driveway — an hour from the nearest interstate — I take a deep breath as I put my sedan in low gear for the climb to her house. When she bought her land, the only path to the top of the steep slope was an old skidder road, a remnant of the wooded property's past use as the raw material for a nearby lumber mill. Although the excavators who prepared Kathe's home site have made it less of a ski jump than the original, the car balks at the last steep climb, and I back down the driveway to wait.

space: 3,700 square feet • **best deal:** bathroom tile — 50 cents a square foot • **time to complete:** 17 months • **key accomplishments:** found my land; chose the house site; confronted each challenge with a cool head.

Tall front windows offer expansive views toward the mountains.

Kathe Higgins

View from the master bedroom, in a loft space above the main floor. One of her workmen, Mike Putnam, made the railing as a Christmas gift for Kathe.

Kathe arrives in a four-wheel drive to load bags and equipment, and takes us easily to the top. The front of her house, with its soaring windows and bowed front, capped by an angel weathervane, bears a striking resemblance to the prow of a ship. The sun is shining and the view is breathtaking.

But it took Kathe much more than a jaunty ride in an SUV to settle here.

The Design

When Kathe married, she moved into her husband's house, which was heated with electricity and not well-insulated. The couple spent a great deal of money converting to propane heaters and a woodstove — an expensive but ineffective fix. At the same time, a chill had settled on their marriage.

As the relationship floundered, Kathe sought help from a counselor, who asked her what she thought would happen next. She remembers:

"I closed my eyes and saw myself walking up a steep hill with a suitcase in my right hand, heading toward a house with a lot of windows. When my husband and I finally decided to divorce, he brought home some catalogs of house plans. Neither one of us wanted to stay in the house we'd shared. I picked one up and the page fell open to the house that I'd seen in my mind's eye, years before, when I'd talked to the marriage counselor. I went through all the catalogs, but nothing came close to that first one. So I ordered the plans. It's the design on which this place is based."

Her experience with big energy bills led her to investigate building with straw bales — a natural material with excellent insulating properties that has only recently started to gain acceptance in the cold Northeast climate. Finding an architect to tweak the catalog plans for layout and the requirements of strawbale, she began to pull her ideas together.

She wanted lots of light and a large volume of high-ceilinged space; the design accommodates this with a bank of tall windows to the southwest,

Left: Looking east from the great room. Below: Once the house was framed, construction meetings — with lunch provided by Kathe — took place around a strawbale table.

which provide spectacular sunset views. She placed the master bedroom and bath in a loft space above the main public rooms, so that her bedroom would share this view.

Because Kathe has always loved animals, she has plenty of her own — five dogs and a cat. She added a mudroom off her kitchen that combines a laundry and powder room. It's a great spot for bathing the dogs when they come in wet and muddy from outdoors.

Actually, the design was the easiest part of the journey. The real challenges appeared nearly as soon as she began to build.

The Climb

"I made plenty of mistakes. Because the home I had shared with my husband sold immediately after our divorce became final, I needed to act quickly on the next steps. I had to move into a short-term rental — the only one I could get, as I have so many pets. This gave me a tight window for building.

"On the recommendation of my site contractor, I hired a general contractor without really checking personally with his customers. Even though I had the plans and the land, and had finished the estimating and was prepared to do the purchasing of most of the materials that went into the house, the bank granted me a construction loan on the condition that I hire a GC instead of supervising the project myself. Accepting those terms was a very costly error on my part."

With the contractor's promise to finish the job before her rental expired, all went well for awhile, with the exception of occasional clashes between Kathe and her builder. Waiting for disbursements from the bank, Kathe tried to keep the project moving by ordering and paying for materials herself — with her credit cards.

She never expected the contractor to leave the job unfinished, with all of her loan money gone

and not fully accounted for, and with thousands of dollars in credit card debt. It was a frightening position to be in. But she prevailed.

Hiring her contractor's employees, whom she had befriended as she worked beside them on the first stages of construction, the two men, Kathe and another friend completed the house. With the lease on her rental expiring and the house less than half finished, she lived on-site until the work was complete — not comfortable, and certainly not fun. It was a trial by fire, as she learned to do things she'd never done before, like tiling all the floors herself.

"The people at the tile store gave me a quick lesson, and I was off. I made the dreadful mistake of laying tiles in flannel pajama bottoms and kneepads. Tile adhesive and grout draw the moisture from your body, so the result was very dry and cracked skin — all over.

The custom base and chairs for Kathe's glass-topped table were made by a local metal artisan.

"A better approach — now that I know better — is to drink lots of water and take horsetail or something with silica in it to maintain skin elasticity. And wear mud gloves and heavy sweat pants!"

Every step of getting the house closed in and finished provided a new challenge. But Kathe learned to roll on this bumpy road, drawing encouragement from one of her workers, Mike Putnam, whose memorable refrain, "How do you eat an elephant? One bite at a time" kept them smiling through many a dark day.

Ultimately, Kathe was able to get a mortgage to cover a good portion of the shortfall in funds, although she is still paying off large credit card balances.

"It was difficult, and I would be lying if I didn't say I was scared, but the experience made me a lot stronger," she admits. And her financial hardship brought out the same resourcefulness that had

Left: View from the guest wing to the public areas. Kathe tiled the entire floor herself.

Kathe models her snow-plowing gear — in the same palette as the house.

helped her through many earlier difficulties.

Because the slope to her house is so steep, and most of the major construction was done in the cold-weather months, Kathe learned to plow the snowed-in driveway herself, to get the workers and delivery trucks up to the job site during construction. Strapped for resources to pay the ever-growing stack of bills, she turned this newfound skill into extra cash during New Hampshire's long, harsh winters. She called the advertising department of the local paper:

"WANNA GET PLOWED WITH LILY? Residential snow plowing. Discounted rates for single mums and senior citizens."

Once the ad saleswoman realized that Lily is Kathe's truck — named for the only pooch in her house that will ride in it — she placed the ad and Kathe wound up with seventeen steady customers, and some new cash flow.

Kathe also works from home for a local water treatment business, and her large, full basement will soon be fulfillment headquarters for a friend's mail order business that sells clogs and rubber boots in many sizes and colors. While she still carries too much debt for her own comfort, she is working her way back to a solvent and more serene future.

Colors

"I really didn't like the popular colors of the fifties and sixties when I was growing up: rust, avocado, harvest gold, gruesome greens and browns. The family of one of my good friends dared to be different. They painted their sunroom a warm pastel green with lavender trim. How I loved being in that room! The soft colors and natural light were very comforting to me. So I filed that away for a time when I could have my own place."

Kathe Higgins

Even before her house took shape in her imagination, Kathe would browse through paint samples. Her eyes always seemed to come to rest on a peachy-pink color. "It made me feel almost weightless," she remembers.

This epiphany happened while she was still married, and her husband had given her carte blanche to add her own touches to his house. "Decorating was not his strength," she recalls, "and his house was mostly black, white and brown."

"So I painted our home this warm, soft color. For accents, I used various shades of aqua, lavender, pink and rose. My friends would enjoy coming to my house, especially in the middle of the winter, because they felt like they were in the Bahamas."

It's no surprise that Kathe used the same pastels when her own house was ready for decoration. When you visit someone who lives deep in the forested hills of New England, you anticipate a color palette that mimics this woodsy, rustic terrain. But Kathe's eye for color has made her home a warm oasis, even when the temperature drops below zero – not uncommon in January or February in this

kathe's advice

"Building a house is all about time and money," says Kathe. When she found herself without enough of either, she had to scramble to keep her project afloat. Fortunately, she finished the house, got a mortgage that covered most of the unexpected shortfall and is moving forward. But she has some pointers to keep others out of the same uncomfortably hot water.

- I did not get construction financing until I ran out of my own money, and used credit cards to pay for building while I waited for approval from the bank that agreed to grant me a loan. The bank forced me to use a GC, even though I'd done much of the estimating, planning and ordering myself. Get your construction loan approved first (see chapter 16), get it on terms you can live with and never try to pay for your project with credit cards.
- Always check your contractor's references. Speak personally with homeowners about their experiences with him or her. Visit references' houses, and keep digging. Someone is bound to talk if there have been problems. Too late I discovered that the experience I had with my GC was not unique.
- Don't get cornered by time. Building a house takes nine months – sound familiar, ladies? – or longer. It was a mistake to think I could finish mine in the four months between the time the contractor started work and the expiration of my rental agreement.

Left, the guest bath.
Opposite, more of Kathe's colorful layout.

part of New Hampshire. Her counterintuitive approach to decorating is a reminder that, trends notwithstanding, the most successful personal spaces reflect the personal choices of their owners.

"I love my home. I love the location, the design, the windows, the high ceilings, the colors and the sense of serenity I feel when I walk through the door. My spirit soars. I adore the openness, and waking up every morning to the outdoors — there are windows in front of and behind my bed. If I happen to go out at night, I leave one light on, and when I drive up, the front of the house is lit so that you can see the bedroom railing. The view is lovely, and it's especially nice to have dinner while watching the sunset. Everyday, I thank God for my home. I am very grateful."

Morgan Irons

HIS . . . AND HERS

"When I climb the path to my little house, I am grateful for this retreat from the world, so quiet."

Morgan and Alan toast each other as they begin building her house.

"WHEN ALAN AND I decided to marry, both of us had been on our own for some time. I was a single parent, and lived with my young son, Nathan. Each of us was used to having personal space. So when we finally moved into his place together, we knew that someday we would build a small, private space for me on Alan's property.

"As time flew by, Alan and I got on so well that my space slipped to the back burner. With careful economies, he was able to quit working as a carpenter and devote himself full time to pottery and sculpture. I gained the freedom to work at what I love – children's literature, the graphic arts, and the theatre.

"Then my parents died, leaving me and my four siblings a small inheritance. I knew it was now or never, as far as my private space was concerned. In 1994, with Alan as master carpenter and me as carpenter's helper, we got started."

space: 500 square feet • **best deal:** my partner and master carpenter • **time to complete:** 4 years • **key accomplishments:** kitchen shelves and tile, and still-to-come things – built-in bookcases and a tea garden which I will do on my own.

Morgan's tiny house and Alan's (left, background), as seen from her garden.

Above: Her mother's cottage teapots sit on the windowsill facing Morgan's garden.

Opposite page: Morgan's stage — where she, her students and theater colleagues audition and rehearse. The space doubles as a sunrise-welcoming dining area.

The Design

Morgan always loved the idea of "cottage." She traces this affinity for tiny, beautifully crafted spaces to a pair of cottage teapots that always sat on a shelf of her mother's dining room corner cupboard. "In fairy tales and English literature there always seemed to be the requisite cottage, with its cottage garden, of course," she muses. When she visited Europe years ago, she fell in love with low, thatched-roof stone dwellings. "And," Morgan smiles as she admits, "small is good, because who wants to spend time housecleaning?"

She also credits her husband's influence. "Alan has a very earthy, solid aesthetic—post and beam, natural wood, shingled roof—which I admire." Looking at the pair's houses from Morgan's tiny jewel of a garden, one grasps the partnership immediately. Each is unique, quite different from the other—but they fit together perfectly.

Her place is diminutive. But even in such a small space—less than five hundred square feet—Morgan has managed to accommodate her three original requirements.

"I wanted a stage for my theatre work, a library for my books, and a beautiful bathing room where I can have a good soak whenever I want," And somehow, within the home's tiny footprint, she has managed to create a space for all of them.

"I pretty much did the floor plan, in consultation with Alan. Some elements, like the hexed bay—where I placed the stage—and the library window seat, were his ideas. Others, like the stage itself, and the upstairs half-wall in my bathing room, were mine."

Construction

From the summer of 1994 through January 1995, Morgan and Alan worked together to install the systems, bringing water and power up from the big house, and running the cottage waste system to the existing septic tank. "We poured the foundation

wooden floor downstairs. Then insulation, Sheetrock, and maybe taping and painting, though I've lost track of what happened when, exactly. We've chipped away at it ever since, as time, energy and money permit."

Morgan's experience as a cabinetmaker helped her with many of the tasks, but there was a bit of a learning curve. "I had shop skills, mainly," she says. "Many of the tools arc very different from what is needed in framing and on-site finish work. Believe me, this house would never have been more than a dream without Alan's superior building talents, and enormous generosity.

and the slab, put up the timber frame for the first floor, installed the second-floor subfloor and stick-framed the upstairs, put in the chimney, and sheathed and roofed the building. We got off that very cold roof just as the January thaw began."

"The next summer, the windows went in, we put on the shingle siding, and I assume we also did the wiring and plumbing, and set the subfloor and

He has a stunning ability to just get it done. He's given me such a gift."

Under Alan's direction, however, Morgan was able to work at many tasks. "I learned to cut mortise-and-tenon joints and set in wind braces, using drill, mallet and chisel.

"I mostly left the skill saw (circular saw) work to him—I hate that tool, it's too heavy. I drilled and

A massive frame for the tiny house, right. Below: Alan works on the complicated roof.

pegged the frame, nailed up sheathing boards, nailed down subfloors, planed beams with a power plane and routed chamfers (the finish detail on beam edges). I also hung, taped and sanded Sheetrock—work I'm good at—and cut tile for the floors."

Morgan also learned a great deal about her own limits. "I knew enough to conceive the design, but not necessarily enough to execute it. And toenailing (see page 117), a basic task when you are stick-framing, made me so frustrated. When alone, I've been known to scream and beat a piece of wood to splinters with my hammer!"

Details

Having a small space to work with can be limiting; one must be clear about priorities. But having fewer of the elements that cost a lot—doors, windows and plumbing fixtures in multiple bathrooms—allows a builder to lavish attention on personally meaningful details.

Morgan was quite certain about what she wanted, and has slowly worked to achieve the space she envisioned. "I love beautiful fixtures and hardware, and they are expensive.

So it's taking time to be truly 'finished.' You'll notice that many of the lights in the house are not yet fixtured; I still have simple porcelain bulb sockets in many places. I like them much better than a cheap substitute for something that I would really enjoy living with for the long term."

One spectacular detail of Morgan's cottage is the front door, which of course needed to be done so that she could move in. She milled a single

Morgan built the shelves in her tiny kitchen to display many family treasures. Below: hand-wrought door hardware.

of ancient trees, was made according to Morgan's own design. "We both love trees," she says, "and even though this cost a lot and took two tries, with two different artisans, I think the result is worth the effort."

8/4" x 18" x 14' pine plank, which she then cut into four pieces and glued; Alan cut its distinctive shape and window opening, and she finished it. Its hardware, with strap hinges hand-wrought by a local blacksmith to look like the limbs

Guiding Spirit

"Obviously, Alan was my mentor for this project. But I must also express gratitude to my parents; the start-up money for this house came from them. Often, my mother's spirit is with me here. I know she would have delighted in this space, and oh, how she could have used it in her own life! She and my father helped provide it, though he would not have understood the need.

"So many of the decorative details reflect my mother's and my shared tastes: yellow curtains, flowered tablecloths, Spode dishes—they are hers that you see on the kitchen shelves—books and plants. I speak with her often as I handle her treasured possessions—some of which came from her mother—which were packed away for many years."

Personal Pleasures

In her cozy cottage, Morgan has crafted a very personal and private home that many a multitasking mom or overextended executive would envy. And she knows, and appreciates, her little domain.

"I love the natural wood. I enjoy the juxtaposition of massive elements in a small space: heavy

morgan's advice

Like several other home makers in this book, Morg constructed her house over a period of many years — more than a decade — and the process continues. This experience has given her ample opportunity to reflect on her decisions: what worked, and what she'd think about more before moving ahead. Here are a few of her pointers:

- Fantasize about how you'd like to spend time in your house. Be honest about who you are and what you need. As I mentioned earlier, I was so eager for "a room of one's own" — the privacy, quiet, ability to function according to my own rhythms, uninterrupted creative time — that I forgot that I am also, at times, a very social animal. I enjoy having company, and I did not plan my space for gatherings, but only for solitude. If I were to start over from the beginning, I'd place the stairway on an exterior wall to open up the space. That way, I could have more than a few guests at a time, and they would have a place to sit comfortably and see each other. It's pretty tight here!
- If money is tight, prioritize. Don't be practical — feed your soul! A bathtub may be more important than a kitchen stove, unless cooking is your passion, of course.
- For houses and gardens, keep it small! You'll focus on what's important and spend less time cleaning and weeding, and more time enjoying. But even if you think you're ready to shed all unnecessary clutter, build in storage space!
- Don't be in a rush to finish. As you live in the space, you'll learn more about how you want to use it. You can then change your finishing plans accordingly.

Left: *A unique and complex roof profile and dramatic entryway give the tiny space great character*

beams, twelve-inch floor tiles, the plank door. I love the natural light, the view of the garden and the back field, the maple tree by the path which my son dug in the woods for my Mother's Day present when he was thirteen. I love having a stage, a library, and a bathing room where I can relax and feel luxurious. I love having things around me that evoke wonderful memories and positive emotions. They are in sight wherever I turn—favorite books, my mother's dishes, my partner's pottery, pictures of our son—Alan adopted Nathan a few years after we were married.

"When I climb the path to my little house, I am grateful for this retreat from the world, so quiet. It is a place where I can function according to my own rhythms, which tend to be extremes . . .working through several eighteen-hour days on a project deadline, unaware of any other schedule. Or, reading through a day and night because the book is too good to put down, and so nothing productive gets done.

"I keep an antique alarm clock with no hands on the bay window sash. This was a gift from Alan when the house was getting close to being finished. He understands my need for unstructured time, even though he is the opposite extreme, almost always on a schedule. Needless to say, we've long since given up trying to do Christmas shopping together!"

One of Alan's sculptures, "The Wanderer," keeps watch at the path to Morgan's house. Another nameless figure sits in front of his place (right).

Pioneers

TWENTIETH-CENTURY HOME MAKERS

Here are just three tidbits about female designers and builders who were ahead of their time.

EVEN THOUGH THE RANKS of the construction trades and the architectural profession have been predominantly male through most of the last century, this doesn't mean that women never held a hammer or sat at a drafting table until some moment in the past thirty years. Here are just three tidbits about female designers and builders who were ahead of their time.

Early in the twentieth century, **Leila Ross Wilburn**, a young woman from a genteel Atlanta family, began her practice of residential design as the second licensed female architect in the state of Georgia. Although she never received the large commercial commissions that her male peers attracted, Wilburn did business for more than three decades, designing houses for middle-class families. The house plans she created and published show a keen understanding of the need for storage space and order, at a time when homes were modernizing with conveniences that we take for granted today. The Wilburn plans have many features that their owners still appreciate: built-in, drop-down ironing

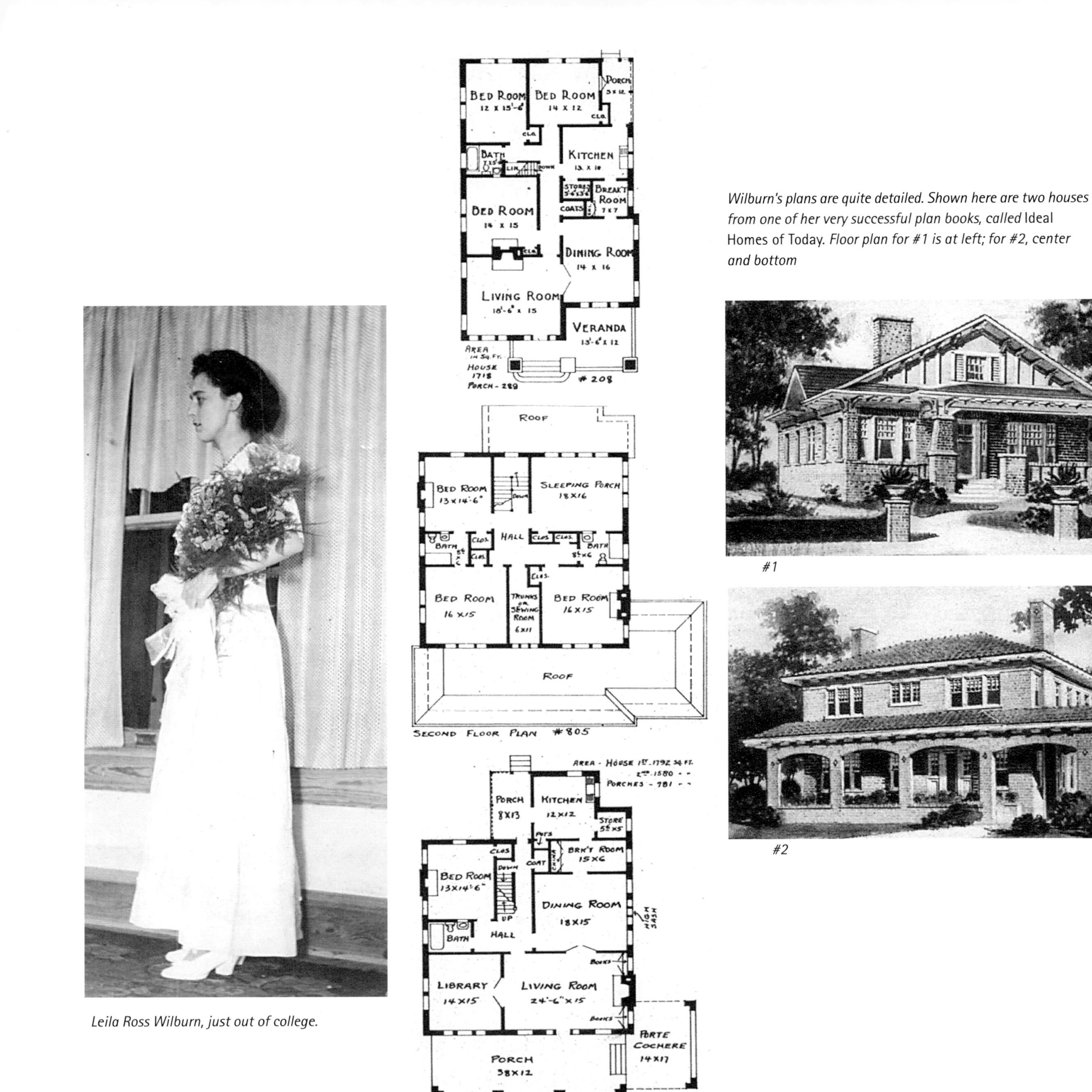

Leila Ross Wilburn, just out of college.

Wilburn's plans are quite detailed. Shown here are two houses from one of her very successful plan books, called Ideal Homes of Today. *Floor plan for #1 is at left; for #2, center and bottom*

#1

#2

boards, glass-doored china closets, and pantries. Today, hundreds of Wilburn-designed homes line the streets of old Atlanta neighborhoods. They are widely sought after by modern buyers for their functional design and aesthetic appeal.

Anyone familiar with the back-to-the-land movement of the 1960s and '70s will probably recognize the names of Scott and **Helen Nearing**, who became living models of self-sufficiency and an organic approach to health and nutrition for a generation of counterculture homesteaders. Leaving the city in 1932 to test their ideas in rural Vermont, their book *The Good Life* (Schocken Books, 1990, reprint ed.) chronicles the couple's hands-on experience with home building, gardening and living well with a lot less than most people can imagine.

Helen was the designer and contractor/builder of both Nearing homesteads, the first in Vermont, and the second compound at Harborside, Maine. The second house, shed and outbuildings—built when Helen was in her seventies, and Scott was in his nineties—have walls of local stone. Helen not only designed the buildings, but also set every stone herself. The homebuilding process was chronicled in *Our Home Made of Stone*, which Helen also wrote (out of print, Downeast Books, 1983). The couple lived at Harborside together until Scott's death in 1983 at the age of 100; Helen died in 1995 at the age of 91.

Having chosen a site with a beautiful prospect, left, Helen Nearing — in her seventies — selected and set every stone for her home and outbuildings at Harborside, Maine.

Both the Vermont and Harborside homes are now open to the public, under the direction of the Good Life Center, a nonprofit foundation established by Helen just before her death to continue the Nearings' work. Volunteer stewards live on and maintain the properties and gardens.

As a child, **Emily Muir** spent hours lying on the floor drawing pictures of animals, of people, of fantasies . . .and house plans. In the 1930s, her parents purchased a large parcel of shore land on Deer Isle, Maine, where the family had spent summers for nearly twenty years. While the property included an old farmhouse, her mother had it torn down. She replaced it with a family home by the water, for which Emily drew the plans—the first of more than thirty houses she would build, along with fifteen renovations, on the island. Using materials from her parents' dismantled farmhouse, Emily also built a studio for herself and her husband, Bill; she later expanded the work space into a year-round house.

The Muirs took up full-time residency in 1939.

At the age of ninety-eight, Emily published a memoir, *The Time of My Life* (Island Institute, 2002), which recounts some of her experiences as artist, architect, devoted civic volunteer, and environmental and social activist. Although she died in 2003, just months shy of her hundredth birthday, she is warmly remembered by all who knew her.

Without formal training as an architect, Emily's houses nonetheless combine an appreciation of their beautiful surroundings with floor plans and features that are functional and comfortable. Her first subdivision, on one of the island's striking western coves, displays her sensitivity about preserving the location's natural beauty, predating by decades the current sustainable development and green building movements. She was careful about guarding the landscape; many current summer residents do not even know that this beautiful little neighborhood exists. So thoughtfully are the houses set on the granite ledges of the property that they are barely visible from the ocean they face.

Once discovered, however, these homes are coveted for their remarkable surroundingps and seamless coexistence with the natural world. An "Emily house" is indeed a treasure.

Emily Muir was so careful not to disturb the surrounding trees and shrubs that her houses are barely visible from the water, and equally difficult to find on land. The house shown, which she named "Wing on Wing," is so successfully camouflaged, and so angular, that it cannot be captured on film in its entirety. Instead of railing, Emily commissioned local fishermen to weave the same type of netting that they use for their lobster traps; this provides a strong barrier, and no one has ever fallen off one of Emily's decks!

a home maker's guide

This poem is one of many wonderful compositions about the building life, published in *Covering Rough Ground*, which poet Kate Braid wrote during her tenure as a journeywoman carpenter in Vancouver. The collection won the Pat Lowther Award for best book of poetry by a Canadian woman. In addition to her years spent as a carpenter, Kate has also been a secretary, a child care worker and a lumber piler. She now teaches writing in British Columbia.

"Against all odds, women can do anything that men can do . . . Men may be stronger physically, but that just means that women need to be creative about how to get the job done."

—Lizabeth Moniz

Woman's Touch

Lunchtime, sitting on a lumber pile
in the middle of the construction site,
my eye fell on Sam's 32-ounce hammer
with the 24-inch handle.

How come all our tools
are longer than they are wide?
I asked.

Silence.

Feeling reckless
with confidence because
that morning I'd cut
my first set of stairs
at a perfect fit, I pushed on.

How come the hammer,
the saw, everything
except the tool belt looks like
you know what?

Don't be so sensitive, Sam said.
How else could they be?
There was a chorus of grunts
in the bass mode.
Besides,
Sam was on firm ground now,
the circular saw is round.

Ed raised his head slowly.
The circular saw was invented by a woman,
he said, and took a bite of salami.

He finished the meat then sat
quite still, contemplating his Oreo.
In 1810 in New England, he continued,
Sarah Babbitt's husband had a sawmill
where they cut the logs over a pit
with a man at each end of a huge hand saw.
She noticed they wasted half
their energy, for hand saws only cut
on the push. She had an idea.

Ed took a chocolate bite and chewed.
Even Sam was quiet.
She went into her kitchen,
fetched a tin dish and cut
teeth in it. Then she slipped it
onto the spindle of her spinning wheel,
fed a cedar shake into it
and the circular saw was born.

Ed folded his brown paper bag.
After a certain silence
Sam spat.
I knew there was something funny
about that saw, he said
and sulked off stomping sawdust.

—*Kate Braid*

Learning the Basics

BUILDING 101

THE FIRST STEP TOWARD getting hands-on with a house is to learn about the tools and techniques of the building trade. To borrow a phrase from musicians' slang, you have to earn your chops—pay your dues, put in your time. There are many ways to do this, including trial and error, but an unsupervised workout with a reciprocating saw is not something anyone who knows this stuff would recommend.

Better to learn from the pros. All kinds of opportunities exist to learn woodworking and building skills (see "Building Lessons," chapter 17), and in the spring of 2004 my photographer and I made the trek to Yestermorrow Design/Build School in Warren, Vermont, to follow a class through a basic building course, taught by a female instructor who has been a carpenter for many years.

Checking plans: the class discusses the work ahead as they examine the architect's drawings for the project.

Orientation begins after everyone arrives on Sunday afternoon. Students and instructor Patti Garbeck introduce themselves. The group has signed on for a variety of reasons:

Lee owns a small house that needs extensive renovations. She has done some carpentry tasks before, but wants to learn enough to attempt her home rehab on her own.

Nancy is a grandmother, retired and recently remarried. Her goal is to build a play cottage for her granddaughter. She passes around a photo of the playhouse site, which is graded and ready; now is her chance to learn to design and make the structure. "Using tools and building something are two of those thousand things I'd like to do before I die," she says.

Gina is in the process of contracting a house of her own not far from the school. Although other people will be doing most of the work, she wants to familiarize herself with the process and

The class: from left, Nancy, Lee, Terry, Alicia and instructor Patti Garbeck. Gina was on her way.

"get comfortable." "I'd like to work beside the builders on some stuff," she says.

Alicia is renovating a house with her partner. "I don't really know anything about carpentry or building, but I'd like to learn. Hiring others to do the work is very expensive; I'd like to do a lot of it myself."

Terry has already taken Yestermorrow's Power Tools for Women weekend course. Encouraged by that first venture, she wants to learn more basics.

Yestermorrow was founded in 1980, growing from one tiny building to a sprawling campus, much of it constructed by successive classes of students, who sign on to learn not only basic carpentry, but also specialized building skills such as timber framing and strawbale construction. The school's wooded site is dotted with cottages and other structures that serve as classrooms as well as hands-on building laboratories.

The women's class will tackle the reframing of the ground-floor interior of the school's original classroom building—a chalet-like structure that is somewhat the worse for wear. Because the school needs housing for its instructors and interns, the women will frame up a couple of small lodging rooms.

Patti has drafted a list of tasks that the students will try to complete within the week. But the first order of business is the safety drill.

After the safety instruction, the students learn about their tools. Everyone has brought some basic equipment from home, including measuring tapes, hammers and squares.

ABOUT FASHION, AND SAFETY

"Eyes, ears, fingers, toes," should be the handywoman's mantra. Remember that you want to keep all of yours intact.

Body protection is a must when using tools; most professional carpenters can show you at least one scar left by an accident that was a result of their own carelessness. Here are some basic rules to follow:

Ear and eye protection — safety must-haves.

Wear sunscreen when you work outside. Leather is for library chairs, not your face.

Tuck it in or take it off. Leave dangling earrings and flowing sleeves in the closet. Wear comfortable clothes that fit close to the body; they won't get in the way of power tools, and won't snag on the materials you're working with. Put your beautiful long hair under a cap, secure it away from your face with a clip or tie it in a ponytail or braid.

Protect your eyes with safety glasses or goggles. For those of us of a certain age who need magnification at close range, it's not necessary to wear reading glasses under the safety specs; instead, look for goggles with built-in diopters that match your required strength. Companies now make safety eye protection in a variety of styles; don't forget to select UV-screening goggles for working outside.

Safeguard your ears with a pair of sound-deadening earmuffs or earplugs. In millions of homes across the country, the wives of retired carpenters have to scream at them across the dinner table, and the TV is tuned loud enough for folks in the next county to hear. That's because for many years, no one paid attention to the real hearing loss that can result from continual exposure to high-decibel power tools and building equipment.

Wear work gloves when handling rough lumber. It used to be tough to find small sizes for the female hand, but manufacturers are learning to make them, and most hardware centers now stock them. Use rubber gloves, or disposable latex gloves when working with wood adhesives, or other liquids and solvents that might irritate skin.

Under NO circumstances should you wear soft shoes or sandals when doing building and carpentry work. Invest in a good pair of sturdy boots and comfortable socks that wick away moisture. Professionals prefer steel-toed boots, as these are the best defense against the damage that a dropped hammer, errant nail or stack of lumber can inflict.

Finally, never try to tackle a project when you're tired, hungry, upset or all of the above. Fatigue and distraction are a primary cause of building-related accidents. This work should be satisfying and fun. If you don't feel up to the task at hand, take a break.Always ask for help when you don't know what to do next.

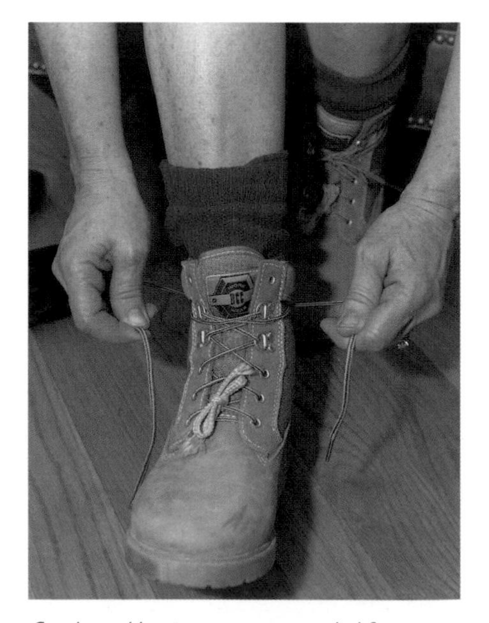

Steel-toed boots are recommended footwear. Personalize with pink laces, if you wish.

The Long and Short of It

"Measure twice, cut once." –Traditional carpenter's motto

If you've ever watched professional contractors wield a measuring tape, it's analogous to a cowboy with his lasso—a fluid, natural movement that's the product of years of experience. In Patti's class, the motions are slower, more deliberate.

The little tick-marks between the inches—showing quarters, eighths, even sixteenths of inches, are often difficult for novices to call. Is the mark three-eighths? Five-sixteenths?

One solution is to buy a measure with a *fractional read*—which uses real fractions to label those little ticks. Pros know the tick marks without a guide—but fractional tapes are a great idea for the rest of us. Get a 25- or 30-foot tape—the best all-purpose sizes.

As for the carpenter's motto, Patti is more sanguine. "Everyone makes mistakes, so don't make yourself crazy. Remember, if you cut your stock (piece of wood) too short, you can always use it somewhere else."

If I Had a Hammer

Hammers are probably the most personal of hand tools—definitely an item to be tested before buying. "Everyone has different arm strength," says Patti, whose favorite is a Japanese 20-ounce framing hammer with a fiberglass handle. Its head has a sculptural

quality — almost bird-like — and everyone smiles as they try swinging it. It feels good in the hand.

Carpentry chores require a hammer with a bit of heft — at least 12 ounces. A 16-ounce model, with a claw for prying nails, is the most commonly used size. Framing hammers have a longer handle than all-purpose ones — for reaching up or down when nailing a frame that may have an eight- or ten-foot vertical span. Some hammer heads have a waffle face to get a better hold on nails, which is good for framing and other heavy chores.

But smooth heads have a purpose too. "You don't want to use a waffle-face head for a board

that is going to be seen," says Patti. "It will leave checkerboard marks where it hits the wood."

"One of the mistakes people make with hammers is overusing their hand and wrist in the swing." Patti grasps her hammer somewhat low on its handle. "Use your arm, and let the hammer do the work. Otherwise you get sore very quickly, and you don't have the striking force you need. It takes practice to get a feel for it."

Field Trip

After a short workout with the hammers, the students break for a visit to the local lumberyard. Since the work they'll do this week is framing walls, their first chore is to hunt for studs.

No, Samantha, a stud is not the cute salesman in the plaid shirt. A stud is a two-by-four piece of lumber, sold in lengths of eight feet or more, usually soft wood, but not usually two inches by four inches as claimed.

Framing lumber is two-by-four when it's cut from the tree trunk in the mill, but it is usually sold dried and planed, and its real dimensions are one-and-a-half by three-and-a-half inches. This is just one way that traditional nomenclature gets in the way of an amateur's understanding, and confusing when you first attempt to lay out a wall. But all of it is learnable.

To do list.

Selecting good framing studs turns out to be as difficult as discerning the one nice guy in a room full of creeps. Since most lumber now comes from trees that are bred to grow to cutting size quickly, the wood is often much less than perfect. Patti cautions, "Pick out your own lumber, if you can." She pulls out a two-by-four and shows the students how to sight down its length looking for face bends (on the wide

Left: *Learning the technique of driving or removing large nails takes some practice.*

Right: *Nail pulling is a great workout.*

side), called *cupping*; edge curves (on the narrow side) called *crooks*; and the presence of knots across the grain and through the wood's depth, a defect which weakens the lumber's strength.

"There are many reasons why I took the class, hands-on experience being the biggest," says Lee McDavid. *But in the back of my mind I also wanted to be able to walk into my local hardware store/lumberyard and hold my own. Nearly all the women I know who have ventured outside of the paint department can testify to the hostility that can follow you. Most of the men who work in these places seem to be schooled in condescension and ridicule. This has happened to me time and again, although it's beginning to change in some places. I discovered, though, that it helps to know the correct terminology instead of asking for 'that little round thingy.'"*

Toe Nail Dancing

Now it's time to learn by doing. Having acquired the requisite number of studs, the students return to the workshop for practice before framing with the good new lumber. They use short pieces of two-by-four from a scrap barrel to try the art of toe nailing.

To frame a wall, vertical studs are nailed into a floor plate — a long stud that sits on the slab or subfloor, creating the bottom piece of the frame — which defines the length and depth of the wall being framed. To make a good hold between the vertical and horizontal pieces, the nails must be driven through the vertical stud diagonally into the plate. Nailing at this angle grabs more of both pieces of wood and makes a secure joint.

Toe nailing is a tough chore for a novice. The exercise simultaneously turns into a lesson on removing nails — with hammer claws, pry bars, and a delicate-sounding tool with a lot of leverage, called a cat's paw. An hour passes as each woman learns the technique, nailing and then extracting fasteners after they have been toe nailed into fantastical shapes. Bodies bend and sway in a strange workshop

Victory is sweet; after a struggle, Nancy frees a nail.

dance. By noon, everyone is tired and ready for lunch.

Old Saws, and New

Saw orientation gave students some "aha!" moments.

If you've ever used a hand saw and tried to cut wood with both your push and pull movements, it probably perplexed you that the saw whined and stuck and didn't seem to cut very well. If you borrowed your husband's saw, he probably complained that you made it dull. He's right.

Hand saws cut only on one stroke, and those most widely used in the western hemisphere cut on the push stroke, making the process much easier than the push-and-pull battle you may have experienced. Still, sawing on the push is easier for guys and their big biceps.

There is a better way. Japanese hand saws are perfectly designed for women. They look like beautiful but very sharp spatulas, and cut the same way we usually do in the kitchen – on the pull stroke. It is the most graceful cutting tool the students had ever seen. Everyone wanted to use it.

"There is a lot of unnecessary mystery in carpentry. But walls, windows, doors, roofs – are all part of a system that at its core is pretty simple. I never understood how it all went together before." – Lee McDavid

A Japanese saw in action.

Empowerment

Power tools become the moment of truth for a woman who truly wants to do-it-herself. They are loud, the moving parts look scary; they make a lot of us want to run straight to the powder room.

But the truth is that they make a lot of different building and carpentry chores go much more quickly. And once you know how each one works – have held it in your hands with an experienced eye looking over your shoulder and guiding your progress – this equipment is as friendly as your cook stove or your sewing machine, both of which could be dangerous if you didn't know what you were doing. Just find a teacher you trust, use your safety gear, follow directions and ask as many questions as you need to.

It opens the door to a whole new world.

"If you can master a circular saw, you can do anything. And I mean anything. Not just carpentry. Everything else in life seems within reach."

– Lee McDavid

After working with it for a couple of days, the scary power saw becomes just another useful tool.

Elementary Equipment

JILL'S TOOL KIT

WHOLE BOOKS ARE DEVOTED to the subject of tools, so consider this chapter a brief overview. It covers most of the tools a beginner will use, and others that a serious home maker will learn to use as the job demands. It does not cover the big shop tools – band saws and table saws, routers, planers, and other specialized hand and power tools. But even if you never own all of the tools described here, you will know something more about what your contractor, spouse and handy friends are doing when they work on your house.

The Basics: Safety First

Start with safety equipment and the safety guidelines in the previous chapter. Eye, ear and hand protection belong in any tool kit. Protect eyes with *safety goggles*, ears with *safety earmuffs* or *earplugs* with ratings of 25 to 30 decibels for the best insulation from noise. Safeguard hands with the appropriate covering: *disposable gloves* for messy chores like painting and gluing, sturdy *work gloves* with good gripping power for carrying lumber and other heavy items. Include a disposable *dust mask* if you are making sawdust or other debris with particles that might be inhaled. If you are working outside, away from the house, a small *first-aid kit* with sterile wipes, antiseptic cream, bandages, and gauze for small cuts and scrapes belongs in your toolbox or bag.

What Tools Do

Although a carpenter, cabinetmaker or other tradesperson may have hundreds of tools, you may have only a kitchen drawer full as you begin a collection. Think about tools in terms of function; buy the basics for the jobs you are doing, and add to your kit as you gain confidence, and as the job requires. Building and repair require *measuring* and *marking, cutting, joining, fastening* and *finishing.* If you have to take apart or clear an area before you build or repair, *demolition* is also part of the task. And since your hands will most likely be occupied, you will need one or more devices for *holding* the materials you are working on. Most tools will fall into one of these eight categories; some will fulfill more than one function.

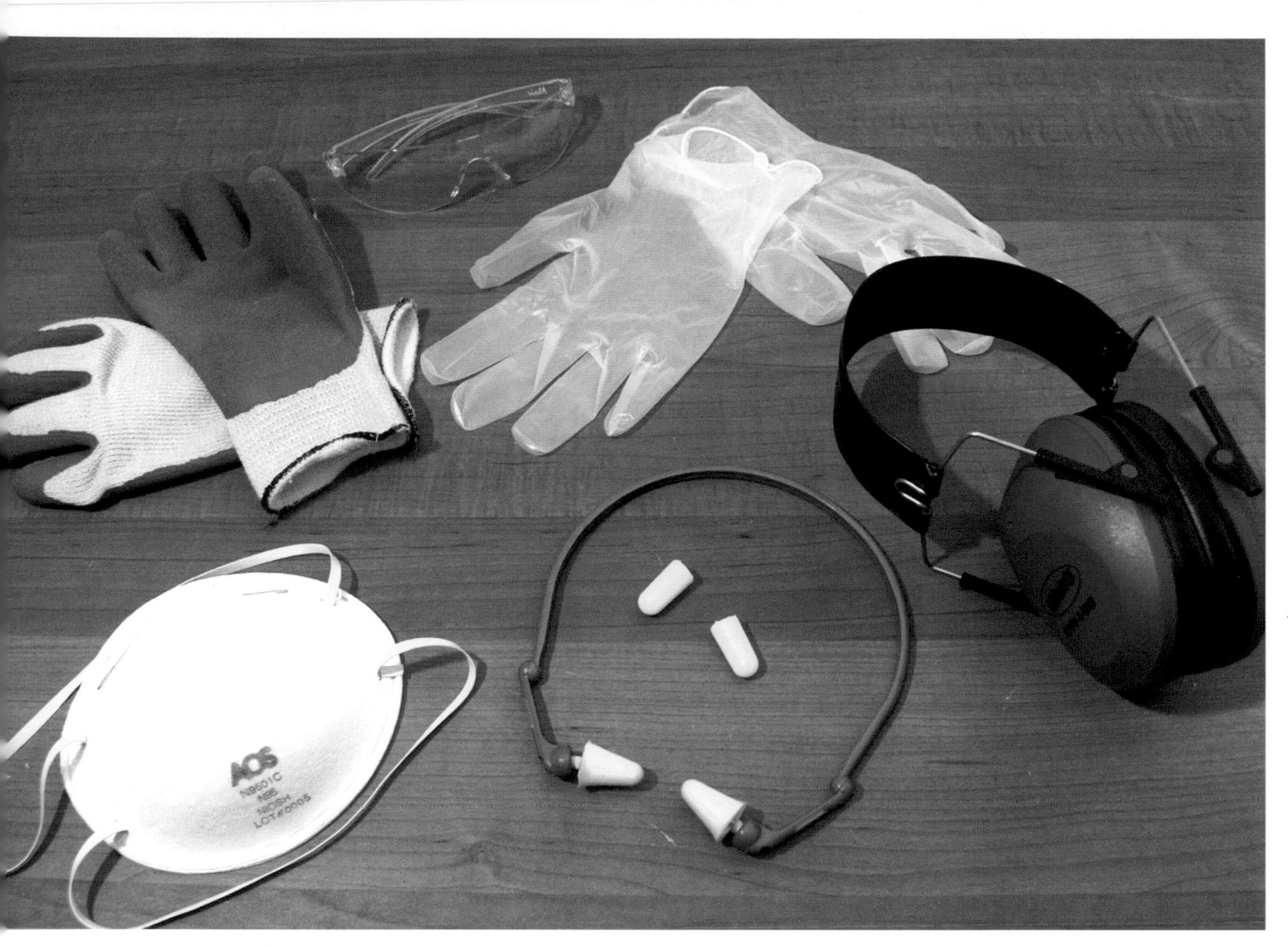

Clockwise, from upper left: work gloves, goggles, latex gloves, safety ear muffs, earplugs, dust mask.

How to Choose

Buy tools that feel good in your hand; you need to be comfortable. – Patti Garbeck

This carpenter's advice is important. Try to handle the tool before you buy it. Do you like the grip? Does it fit your hand and arm strength? Does it feel sturdy, but not too heavy? Find the home center, hardware store or lumberyard where the staff is friendly and helpful. Be specific about what you need to do, and let them show you a few options.

Sometimes tools come in large, inexpensive sets, with some things you need and others you don't. Try to avoid these. When it's made of better materials and has a lengthy warranty, a tool will be more expensive than its bargain-price competitors. But quality tools can last a lifetime, so get the best you can afford.

Good power tools can be very expensive. Keep in mind that if you need a tool for a limited time and a specific job, you can usually save money by renting what you need.

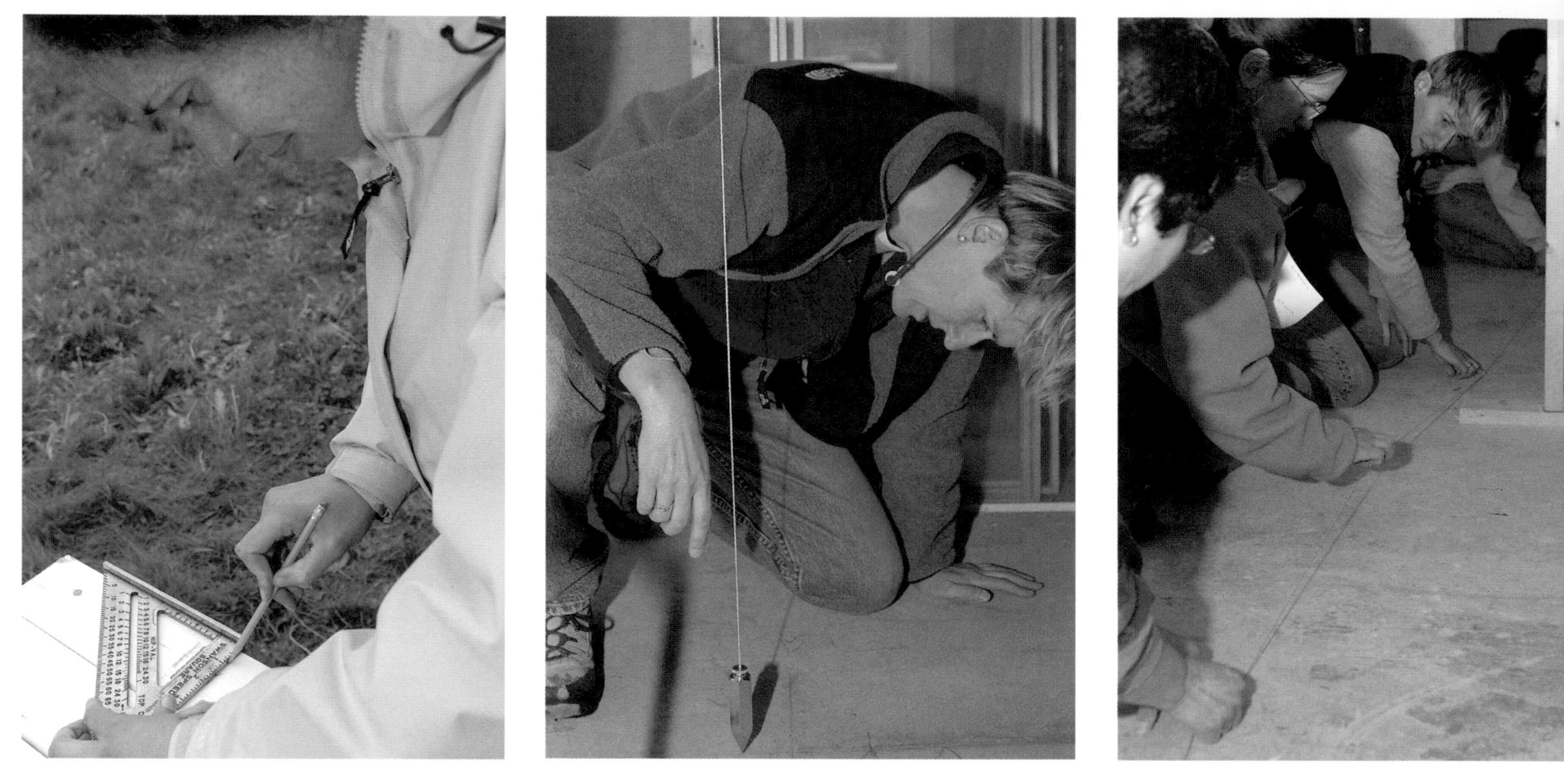

From left: speed square, plumb bob, snapping a chalkline.

Marking

An ordinary, classroom-variety pencil can mark things, but these have a tendency to roll away. *Carpenter's pencils* have a hexagonal shape, with two broad surfaces and four smaller ones, and can be sharpened with a utility knife; their marks may be too thick for fine woodwork cuts, however. A *mechanical pencil* with standard #2 lead will also work fine. "It depends on what you like," says Lizabeth Moniz. "An ordinary pencil can be tucked behind your ear, though, and then it's easy to find when you need it."

Lizabeth also recommends a *crayon* or grease pencil. "Most wood is better on one face or the other, so mark your wood clearly with a bold mark on its 'bad face,' and you'll know that's the side that you don't want to see on the finished work."

Measuring

A *metal ruler* – 12 to 18 inches in length – will handle most small measuring tasks, fits in a drawer, and will last forever if you don't bend or abuse it.

A retractable *measuring tape* is the best all-purpose tool; for maximum versatility, get a 25- or 30-foot model. Look for one with a *fractional read*, to avoid having to count tick-marks every time you measure. Heavy duty tapes last longer; look for a

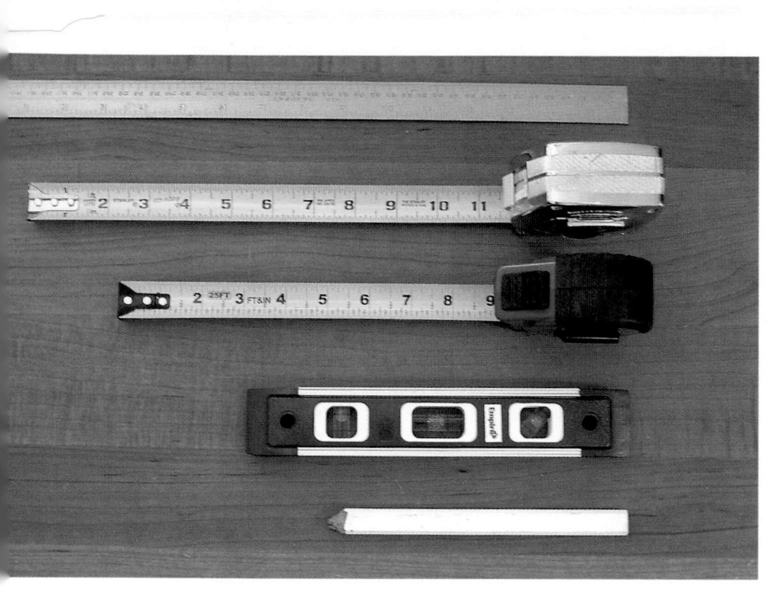

Shown top to bottom: metal ruler, measuring tape, fractional read measuring tape, torpedo level, carpenter's pencil.

locking feature that will stop the tape without having to hold it steady while you measure.

For measuring and marking angles, use a *speed square*, which is also handy for drawing a straight line across a piece of lumber; its lip fits smoothly against one edge (see photo).

Level means something is straight horizontally; plumb means it's straight vertically. To get these measures, carpenters and other tradespeople use levels. When something is out of level, or not plumb, the shape created is distorted (remember geometry?), and subject to all kinds of problems.

Torpedo levels are small — a few inches to a foot long, and are good for small jobs, such as making sure that shelves, pictures, or curtain rods are hanging straight. For larger jobs, levels of two feet or longer are preferred. Traditional levels have a small liquid-filled vial at their midpoint; on longer levels, there are also vials near each end.

When the object is level or plumb, the small bubble in the vial is centered between hatch markings on the vial. Many professionals now use *laser levels* — a more expensive option, but not necessary for beginners with small tool budgets.

A *chalk line and reel* makes it easy to mark a long vertical or horizontal guide on a wall or floor for all kinds of building and renovating chores: laying tile, hanging wallpaper, framing an interior wall. Unlike pencil or pen marks, the guide made by "snapping a line" can be wiped away without a trace.

To line things up vertically (upper and lower cabinets, for example), a *plumb bob* — essentially a pointed weight on the end of a string — can help you find and mark a true vertical line.

Cutting

A *utility knife* can handle lots of small cutting chores. Get one with a retractable blade to prevent mishaps. Utility knife blades look and cut just like razor blades. When you discard a dull blade, wrap it in masking tape so it doesn't nick you, or tear open the trash bag.

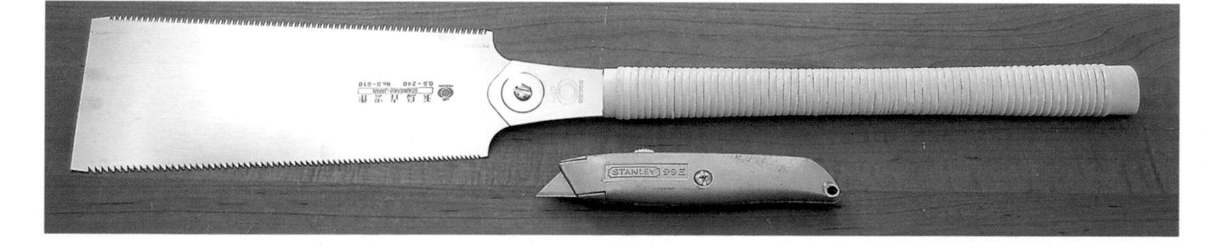

A Japanese ryobi hand saw, with large rip teeth on one edge, finer crosscut teeth on the other; it cuts on the pull stroke. Shown below it is the ever-useful utility knife.

Hand Saws

For modest-sized lumber-cutting chores, a hand saw does the job. Traditional hand saws – called *panel saws* – are 20 to 26 inches in length, and somewhat frustrating for the uninitiated to use. If you want an American-style saw, a *toolbox saw* looks like a smaller panel saw. With a blade that is 10 to 14 inches long, it is easier to cut with, and less susceptible to bending and buckling than the longer panel saw. Unlike the Japanese-style saw (see the previous chapter), it cuts on the push stroke, so the rhythm is push-and-lift, push-and-lift.

Power Saws

A *jigsaw* is a lightweight, easy-to-use power cutting tool that will cut curves quickly and easily. Women tend to love this tool, because it runs like a sewing machine, with a narrow blade that moves up and down rapidly. Many jigsaws feature adjustable blades for cutting on an angle. Jigsaws can also

A well-designed, corded jigsaw.

Tracy sets up her work piece at the chop saw. When cutting, she wears goggles.

make plunge cuts into wood panels (plywood and other sheet goods), so it's easy to make cutouts. Jigsaws are available in corded or cordless models.

The portable *circular saw,* which is often called a Skilsaw™ – the first such product to hit the market years ago – is a reliable, hardworking tool for making straight cuts in wood. If you can only own one power saw for building and remodeling, this is it. Besides learning to control and use this tool properly you need to find the model that feels most comfortable – and one that suits your own needs. Taking classes, and volunteering with a group such as Habitat for Humanity, will expose you to a variety of different models. It's a good idea to try an expensive tool before you buy it.

Circular saws and their cousins – table saws – have spawned a hybrid power saw that has become increasingly popular on job sites. The *miter saw,* also called a "chop saw" by the pros, is a circular saw on a stationary base with an adjustable arm that allows the circular blade to pivot on the base and make straight or angled cuts, accurately, time after time. This accuracy makes the miter saw invaluable when large quantities of lumber must be cut – when framing walls and roofs, for example. The size of the saw blade determines the lumber width a miter saw can cut; the larger the blade, the wider the material it can cut. *Compound miter saws* and *sliding compound miter saws* are further enhancements to the original design and prices rise according to complexity. Miter saws are now available in cordless models, for work away from a power source.

Hammers are an indispensable part of the tool kit. From left, rubber mallet, 16-ounce claw hammer, 15-ounce Japanese framing hammer, tack hammer, urethane carpenter's mallet, 1-inch chisel. Nailsets in three sizes are displayed below the tack hammer.

Joining

I found an all-metal hammer in the street and use it all the time. I like it because it can take a lot of abuse. – Lisa Hawkins

When you build or renovate, the various parts need to come together smoothly, eased or squeezed into place with physical effort and that most important, ancient tool – the hammer – in one of its many forms. Many of these operations involve holding things together with nails, so the right hammer – or set of hammers – belongs in the toolbox.

A small, 7-ounce *tack hammer* is good for small tasks, but you should have a 12- to 16-ounce *claw hammer* for most building and renovation jobs. The claw, which can be straight or curved, depending upon the model, is useful for

MY, WHAT BIG TEETH YOU HAVE! A VOCABULARY LESSON

The teeth on saw blades go in one direction, called the *set* – and this orientation makes a cutting edge, called a *kerf.* The finer and thinner the teeth, the narrower the kerf. Blades are engineered with various numbers of *tpi* – that's teeth per inch. For cuts across the grain, crosscut saws have a higher number of small tpi. Ripsaws – for cutting with the grain – have bigger teeth, and thus a smaller tpi number.

Now you know what contractors mean when they say they're going to "go rip some boards." While it sounds violent, it simply describes the process of cutting wood along its grain.

pulling out mistakes or for taking things apart.

Hammer handles are a matter of personal choice. Wood is traditional, but manufacturers offer a wide range of materials – fiberglass, titanium, and special "anti-vibe" handles to make hammering less tiring on arms and shoulders. *Framing hammers* have somewhat longer handles than all-purpose claw hammers; this feature extends the reach of the tool. Choose the one that feels comfortable and balanced when you swing it.

Sometimes you must hammer nails into materials that could be damaged by the metal head of an all-purpose hammer – a loose floorboard nail, for example. A *rubber mallet* can put the nail back in place without damaging the surrounding wood. When hammering into finish work, carpenters use a *nailset* with a diameter equal to or smaller than the nail head, to drive the nail home or countersink it (hammer it below the surface, then fill the indentation with a plug or wood putty). These handy little tools are sold in packets of various sizes.

In traditional timber framing, parts are joined together with handmade joints. A receptacle is cut into a receiving timber; this is called a mortise. The timber that will join with it has a tenon cut to perfectly fit into this mortise. Sometimes these joints are pegged for additional joint strength. Mortises for pairs of hinges to attach doors to their frames are also cut by hand. For these operations, it's good to have a *chisel* – a very sharp cutting tool assisted in its operation by a *carpenter's mallet* – another hammering device that is made of wood or urethane, and is used to hit the chisel handle and drive its cutting edge into the wood.

Mallets and chisels for timber framing are large, specialized tools, but almost everyone who works on a house will eventually need to install a new door or replace old hardware.

At some point, your tool kit should contain a set of chisels in a couple of sizes, and a mallet that is comfortable for your own strength.

Simple to superior: Driving screws and other fasteners requires a tool that fits the fastener. Shown clockwise from left: combination ratcheting screwdriver, with a range of tips stored in the handle; screwdrivers of different length and tip types; pocket set of Allen wrenches; battery charger and cordless drill driver – a high-end, ergonomically designed model; adjustable wrench.

Fastening

Righty, tighty; lefty, loosey – mnemonic (a memory clue) for recalling the correct direction for tightening and loosening fasteners.

For stopping a leak or connecting one piece of material to another, you need to familiarize yourself with the tools that do these jobs. Screws, nuts, staples, bolts, and washers – all these "little pieces" – have a role in making house parts come together, and apart. Getting them where they belong is the job of fastening tools.

Fastening by Hand

Look around your house. Sheetrock, window frames, small appliances, electrical outlet covers, the case on your laptop – almost everything is held together by screws. Fastening and unfastening is done by means of a *screwdriver,* which can have one of several types of tips, or heads. The Phillips head, by far the most prevalent screw type, looks like a plus sign (+), and comes in various sizes, as does the flat head, shaped like a minus sign (–).

Many manufacturers now make screwdriver sets with ergonomically-designed handles, crafted in soft materials to make holding and turning the screwdriver more comfortable.

Screwdriver shanks come in different lengths – the longer shanks are helpful for reaching recessed screws and some people think the additional length gives better driving power. Other women prefer stubby-shanked screwdrivers that fit easily in a pocket.

Screws can also have hexagonal heads (called set screws). These are commonly used in light fixtures and some door handles, for example, and may be installed or removed with a hexagonal fastening tool, called an *Allen wrench.* You can buy a full set of these in a jackknife-style case, which will enable you to fasten and remove hexagonal screws in a wide variety of sizes.

A convenient, economical alternative to a full set of screwdrivers is a *combination screwdriver.* These handy and versatile tools have a variety of interchangeable screwdriver heads stored in the handle. Some combination drivers have a ratcheting mechanism that makes tightening and loosening easier. For tightening or loosening nuts on materials that are joined with bolts, keep an *adjustable wrench* in your tool kit.

A TIP TIP

Always use a screwdriver with a head that matches the head of the fastener. If you use a too-small driver, you'll lose leverage; too large, and you can strip the screw head. Also, never use a screwdriver for anything but fastening/unfastening screws. Using it as a can lid remover can ruin the tip; you can buy a lid remover for about fifty cents.

This is a small, electric-powered orbital sander designed for finish work; it takes quarter sheets of sandpaper and can be operated with one hand. Full sheets of sandpaper and a foam-cored, disposable hand-sanding black, a four-in-one wood rasp, and metal file are also shown. Power sanders are available in cordless models as well. Large finishing/refinishing jobs require larger, more powerful sanders than the one shown.

Power Fastening

Staple guns are useful for a variety of light fastening chores and power staple guns fitted with heavy duty staples can be used for applying heavier materials such as certain kinds of shingles, for example.

For drilling holes and driving screws quickly and in quantity, nothing beats a *power drill/driver;* it saves both time and wear and tear on your arm and wrist. Like all other power tools, look for a model that is not too heavy and comfortable to grip. The more expensive cordless models with rechargeable batteries can be used anywhere. Look for a power drill with forward and reverse speeds. The better models provide easy adjustments to vary the driving power, or torque.

Finishing

Finish work — all the details that show in a completed space — uses most of the operations described above. But almost all work that shows will need a good going-over with smoothing tools to eliminate visible joints and flaws. *Sandpaper* or *sanding blocks* equipped with the right abrasive — fairly rough sandpaper for removal of lumps and bumps, progressively finer grits for finishing and smoothing between coatings of paint or stain — are a part of the process.

If you have lots of surfaces to smooth, *power sanders* fitted with the right abrasive make the work much faster. Lightweight sanders with a one-handed grip offer good control, and definitely make a smaller job, such as prepping surfaces for new paint, for example, much faster. Professional grade sanders for big jobs — floors, cabinets, countertops — are expensive. These can be rented.

Choosing the right sander requires learning a bit about what each one does. Talk with the retailer about what you're doing before you invest in a sander.

Like cutting wood, sanding raises dust, If you are doing a lot of work with power equipment with dust-collection capability, a built-in dust collection bag or hose coupling that will attach to a shop vacuum is a healthier alternative than letting the debris fly. When you are raising dust, always wear a mask and eye protection.

Lots of small jobs can be accomplished with

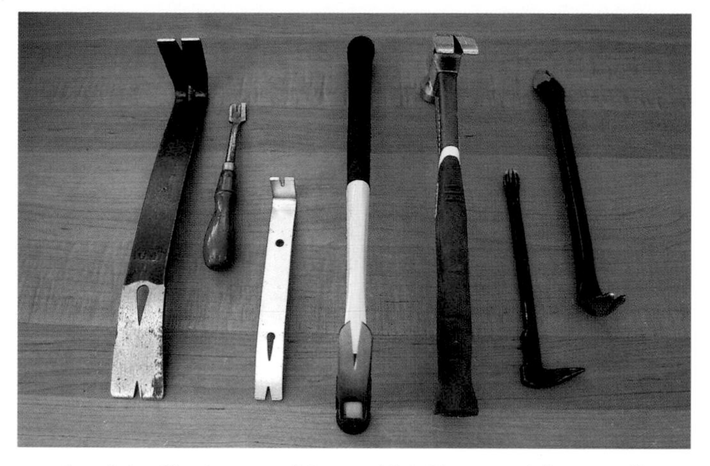

A variety of tools can assist you with taking materials apart. From left, a medium size pry bar, tack remover, small pry bar, framing hammer with claw, regular claw hammer, cat's paws. All these tools provide leverage for breaking up/tearing out material and also sharp "claws" for getting underneath nail heads and easing them out of place.

files. A *metal file* is used to smooth metal parts. Get a file called a *four-in-one rasp* for wood-smoothing tasks; this hand tool has four abrasive surfaces – two on its curved side, and two on its flat side. Files are great for quick work on small areas. Clean out debris from your files with a brass-bristled brush.

Demolition

When you renovate, you usually remove some old work before installing new materials. This means that demolition will figure in your plans. While you may not want to develop your sledgehammer skills just yet, become familiar with the various tools that provide leverage when removing old woodwork, floors, carpets, and so on.

Quickly removing old Sheetrock, cabinets, and other installations of size requires heavier demolition tools – this is where the sledgehammer and a powerful saw called a reciprocating saw will come in handy. Both tools require strength and control (and good safety equipment to protect your body). The *reciprocating saw* – nicknamed Sawzall™ by contractors after the first such tool, introduced and still produced by the Milwaukee Tool Company – has a rapidly-moving straight blade that makes quick work of any job where rough cutting is required. This includes not only demolition, but also making large cutouts, such as window and door openings.

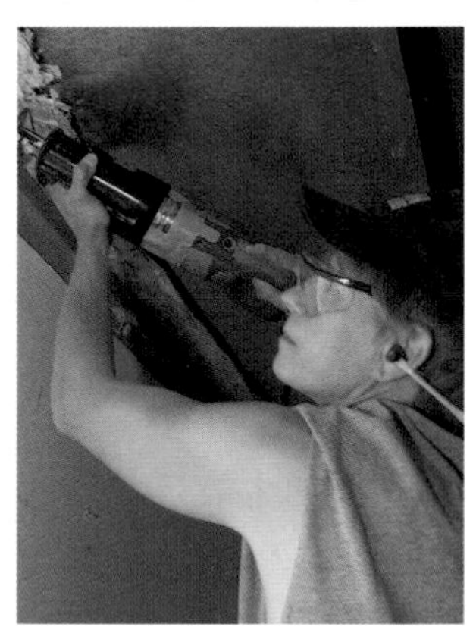

Reciprocating saw.

Bags or boxes for holding and carrying your tool collection are strictly a matter of personal taste. The rigger's bag (upper right) holds dozens of hand tools, and costs less than twenty dollars. For holding a work piece in place, you will want a work table (everything from a portable, foldaway model to a large stationary workbench is available), and clamping devices to hold the materials in place while they are cut, fastened or joined. This photo shows metal bar clamps, spring clips, and locking pliers, all of which provide a "third hand" for your projects.

Making a Design

THE DRAWING BOARD

Where to Begin

IF YOU DREAM OF BUILDING your own house, or just want to renovate the one you already have, take the first step on the path to your goal. Many women in this book began with just a little mind-picture of a "room of my own" – what it would contain, where the windows would be set, what color she would paint it. Visualization is a good place to start.

Inside out: a complicated roof structure can create interesting shapes for "light windows" on the interior. This window faces Morgan's bathing room.

One of my dearest friends, who now lives in Texas, has always kept a three-ring notebook where she files her house ideas. When she was building a home a decade ago, she filled the book with magazine clippings, photos from catalogs, snapshots of rooms and architectural details that she likes – a kind of personal wish book. Many of her ideas took shape; others never came to pass. She has since moved on to another home of her own, but she still keeps a running idea scrapbook to use as time and money allow her to improve the house. You might use a file folder, a big envelope, a basket or a box; the point is to start making a visual catalog of your ideas.

The women whose homes are featured in this book also have good advice for pulling a design together. Here are just a few:

• Carry a tape measure and a little pocket notebook with you, and when you are in a space that you like, measure it, and jot down some notes as

to why it appeals to you. – Lizabeth Moniz

• If you want to build a house, visit the homes of as many owner/builders as you can. Look for things that fit your own wants and needs; take snapshots if it's okay with the homeowners, or make a little sketch. Ask the owners what worked for them and what the problems were. It will help you avoid mistakes when you finally get to building. – Patti Garbeck

Distinctive shingle patterns, applied sparingly, can give a home's exterior a custom look without great expense.

• Designing a home is getting to know yourself. Do you like formal, informal? Plan to give lots of parties, or stay home and meditate? Read books about design and building. I really enjoyed John Connell's book, *Homing Instinct,* which helps you ask yourself the right questions about the space you make for yourself. And when you're ready to draw, take a course at a design/build school. It's an invaluable experience. – Lisa Hawkins

• Be creative! Don't be afraid to put your whole self into the project. Building a home is also building a self – my house is as much a part of who I am now, as I am a part of what it is.
– Alison Kennedy

An interior with exposed framing elements offers opportunities for display and storage.

Designing Women

Many, though not all, of the women whose homes are in this book kept their own drawings of their projects, and very graciously loaned these precious documents to help readers see how the ideas for their houses look on paper. They are duplicated here, as illustrations of the various types of drawings that are used for building. A couple also show the changes that take place in a home as it is built — cross outs and "make dos" when the original idea just doesn't wash.

Most architects will ruefully admit that many of their professional drawings do not materialize in a house that is one hundred percent "as drawn." Changes made by materials limitations, structural problems, building inspectors' quirks and a home-

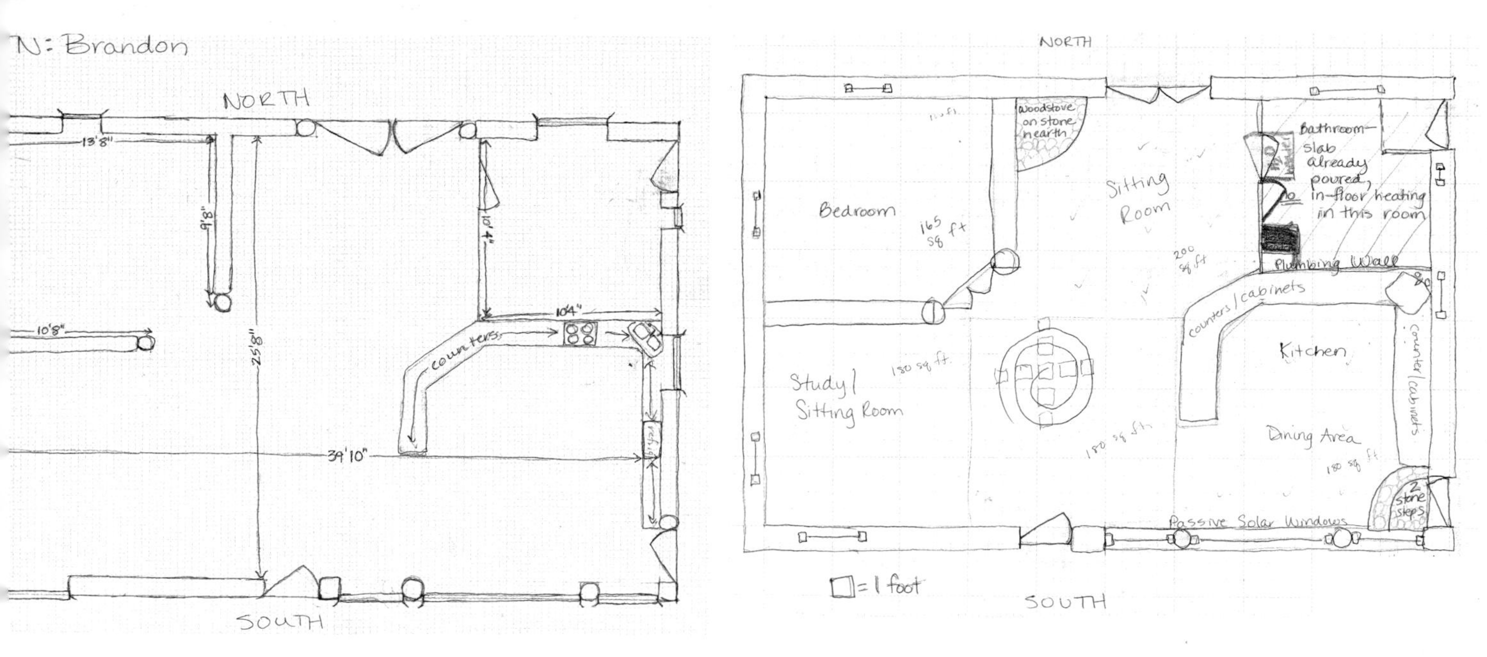

Alison made many floor plans of the interior main floor of her house. The first drawing (left) shows general dimensions; the second (right) gives more detail about square footage and placement of critical design elements. Alison made a large number of floor plans as the project progressed; not included here are system plans (for plumbing and electrical), or other more detailed drawings. "These are early sketches," she says, "and as I refined my thinking and worked with subcontractors and friends who were helping me, I altered certain things. But basically, they show walls, counters, doors and windows in the spots where they are now."

owner changing her mind (beware, that's an *expensive* reason), will all affect what's ultimately built.

Floor Plans

Floor plans are the central element in a set of architectural drawings. They provide the builder and reviewers (subcontractors, inspectors) with key information: the building's configuration, dimensions, interior spaces, circulation and materials.

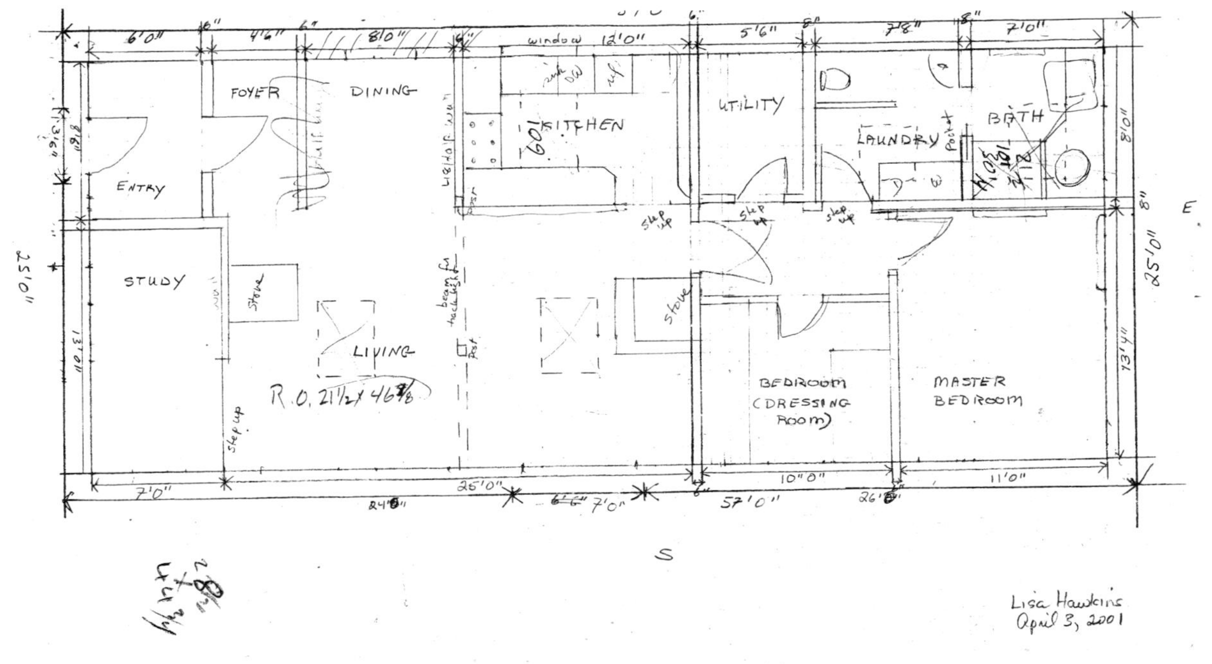

Lisa Hawkins' floor plan is straightforward and carefully measured. While not a professional, Lisa had drawn designs for two previous houses and was more familiar with depicting elements and measurements. In the house "as built," a little wall separating the dining room from the foyer was eliminated; you can see the cross-out on the plan. "Too tight," says Lisa.

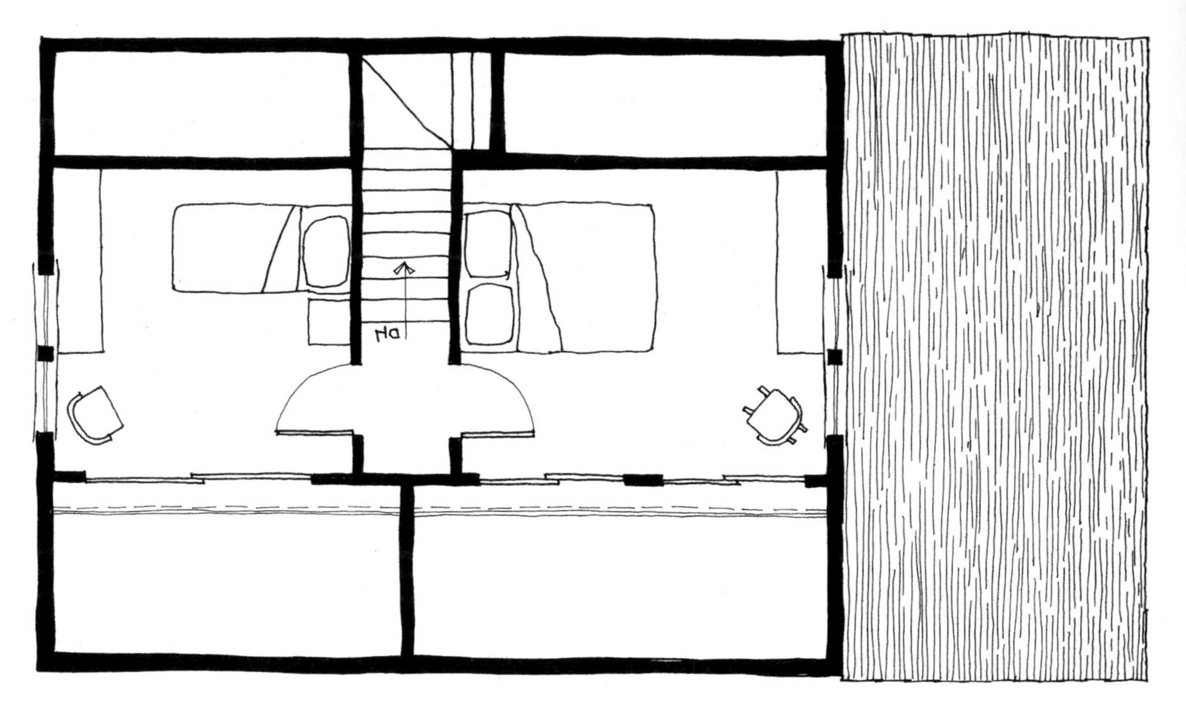

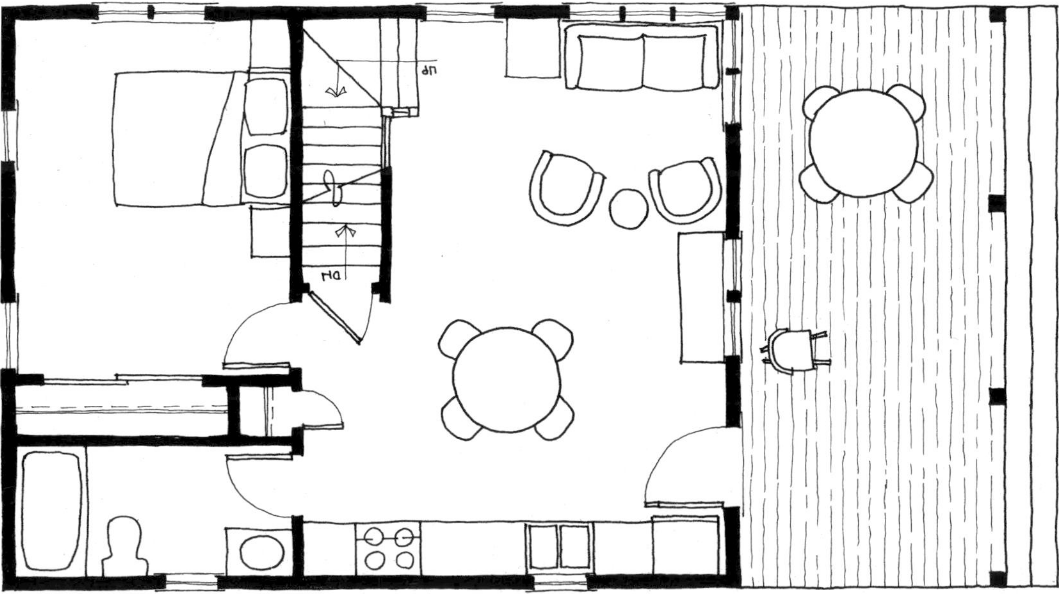

These rough floor plans show the interior of a small unit, with porch, that Mary designed for Pioneer Valley Cohousing Community. This particular rendition shows a first floor with one bedroom (above), and the second floor space (below) divided for two rooms. Some residents chose to keep the upstairs as a smaller loft area, others left the two sides of the second floor more open to each other. "The basic layout was kept simple so that it would be easy to make changes in how it was configured, though kitchen and bath are located similarly in all small units."

Elevations

Elevation drawings can be deceiving. While a real building, viewed straight on, is in three dimensions, an elevation is drawn in only two dimensions. Thus elevations must be read in conjunction with the floor plans so that the building's dimensionality can be understood.

Sections

Siobhan had initially envisioned a stone-faced facade to the left of her front porch. As the house was built, this element was abandoned for budgetary reasons; garage doors are now in its place. Because this front elevation is in two dimensions only, you have to look at her floor plan to get a sense of the sweep of the front stairway.

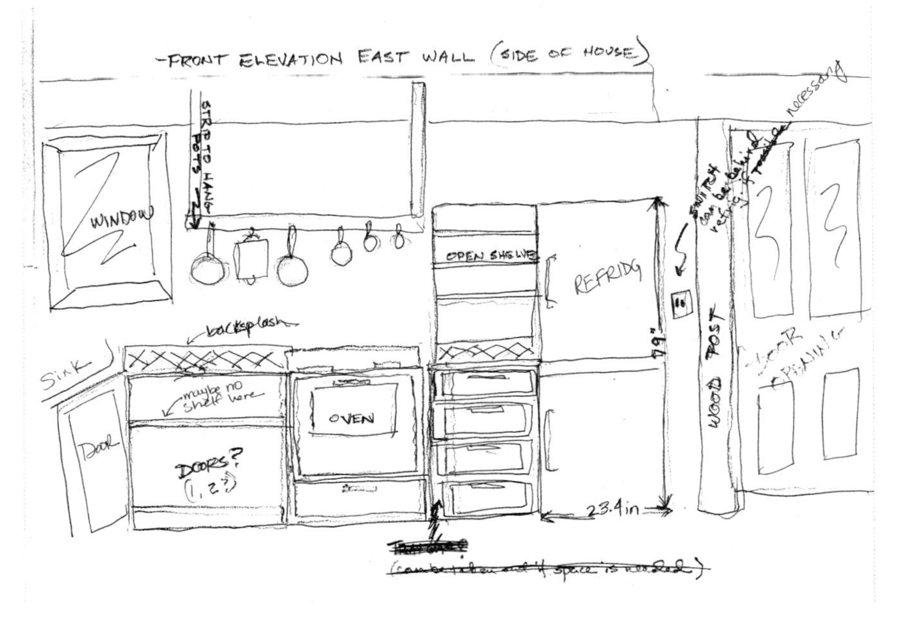

The elevation for Alison's kitchen shows some similarity to the final project, though the final configuration changed a bit. In her broad, quick strokes, you can literally see her "thinking" on the page.

Front elevation for Mary Kraus' small unit plan, showing the porch, steps, gable, and window and door placement.

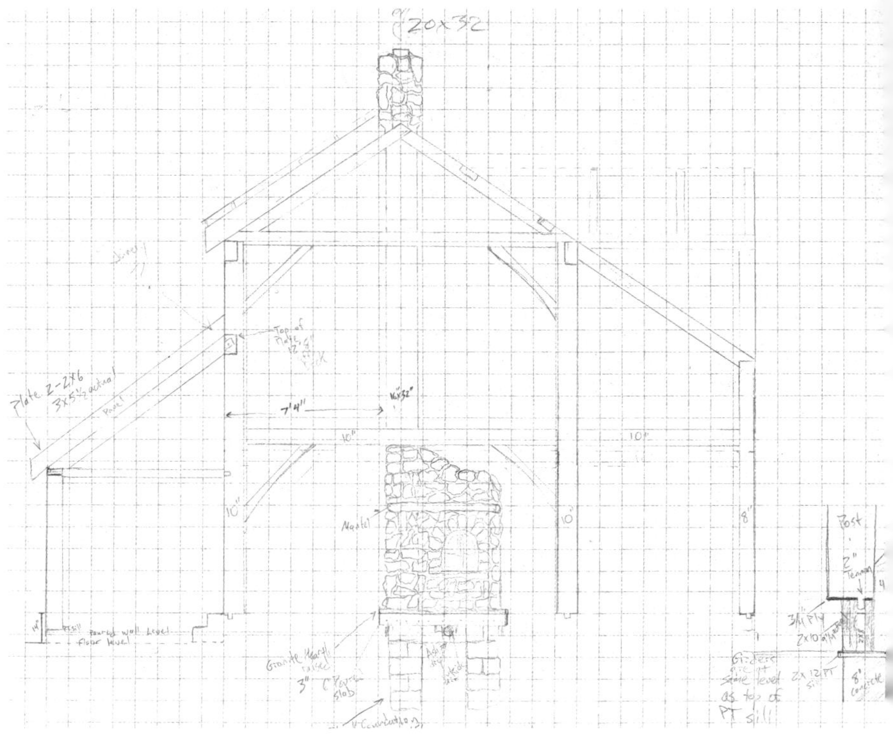

A section of Lizabeth's house, showing the foundation, facade and chimney for the home's masonry heater.

A section generally refers to a vertical cut through a building, illustrating all or a portion of that element.

Systems

Plans for all the systems – heating, cooling, ventilation, plumbing and electrical – must be drawn as a guide for these contractors. The time to detect mistakes is *before* the work is done. In most municipalities – though there are exceptions – system work is subject to inspection. A failed inspection costs lots of time and money.

Siobhan's electrical and plumbing plans were careful and complete. She even made space for an elevator shaft, should a family member or new owner be unable to use stairs in the future. "Put outlets where you're going to use them," she declares. "We decorate our mantels and windowsills for the holidays, so I made sure to put outlets above the mantels and directly under the windows. That way, no cords show. Remember also to put in floor outlets when you'll have tables that need lamps in the middle of a floor."

Perspective

A perspective drawing shows a building or element with dimension, more or less as it would actually look when you are standing in front of it.

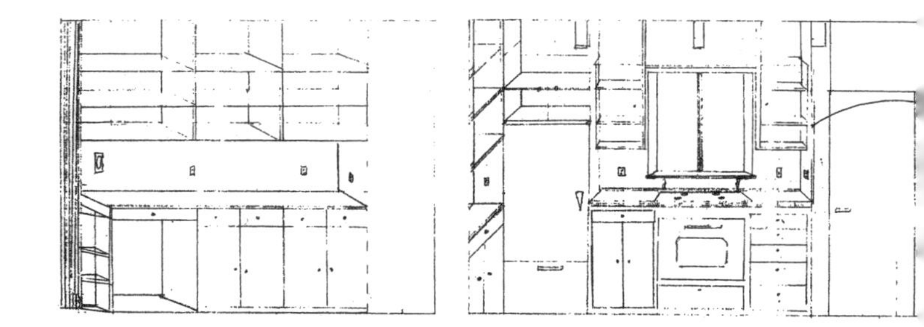

Jill rendered the three walls for her kitchen renovation as she visualized them; she later changed her idea for storage around the stove to a configuration of deep drawers. Island height was raised to accommodate her 6'1" frame.

Using a grid to scale with the dimensions of her roof and the size of the shingles, Alison was able to create an artful pattern with shingles in twenty-four different colors.

Patterns

Should you decide on complex designs for any area of your home – floor tile, decorative mosaics, or, in Alison's case, a multicolored roof – making a pattern will facilitate ordering of materials in the right quantities.

DESIGN HELP

Not everyone has the skills of an architect. Perhaps your home design or renovation sketches never get beyond the "scribble on the napkin" stage. But after thinking about it, you have strong ideas about what you want. Here are steps you can take:

Plan Books Keeping your design ideas in mind (or more conveniently, in a folder with pictures you've pulled from magazines or copied from books), peruse the hundreds of plan books available from the bookstore or library. There are plans for houses of every style and size. You can probably find at least one design that approximates what you are looking for. Plans sell for several hundred to more than a thousand dollars for a complete set; a few hundred more will get you as many plans as you need for building department, contractor, subs and the like. And, with the help of an architect or architectural draftsman, plans can be tweaked for individual needs. That's what Kathe (see chapter 9) did.

Take a Course See chapter 17 for the contact information for design/build schools. For the cost of a full set of pre-packaged plans, you can learn how to make plans yourself. Thousands of people take the plunge every year, and though some end up hiring an architect and a contractor, nearly everyone learns enough to be a better owner/builder.

Hire the Pros Have professionals take your dream in hand and help you make it real. Depending upon your ability to concretely translate your ideas into working drawings, you will need, minimally, the skills of an architectural draftsman for the drawings; the skills of a structural engineer (if you worry your design won't stand up to a building inspector's scrutiny or the local weather conditions); or, finally, the skills of a full service architect, who can give you drawings and certify them as structurally sound.

Architects will cost from about 8 percent to about 15 percent of the total cost of your house or renovation, so these services are expensive. Still, many people who have more resources than time are willing to use professionals to shorten the distance between idea and move-in. It is both a personal and a financial decision.

Finding and Buying Land

THE RIGHT SPOT

WHAT'S YOUR PLEASURE? A cabin in the woods? Mansion in the meadow? Cottage by the sea?

Each of the women in this book had different ideas about the right piece of land. For Alison, a building lot in a subdivision became the site for her desert home. Small and affordable, surrounded by a massive and beautiful landscape, it was a manageable plot for her dreams. Kathe wanted woods and mountains; Patti was content to make a tiny place for herself on a large piece of land. For the women who joined Pioneer Valley Cohousing Community, a vital neighborhood that retained a big dose of natural beauty held a high value.

Finding Property

Which comes first, land or design? Actually, you can start with either. The type of house you want may affect the land you search for. Or, the land you fall in love with, or a piece you already own, may give you ideas about a house.

However, unless you have ready cash to purchase property, having house plans and cost estimates ready may help you get financing more easily. Banks will not grant a mortgage for undeveloped ("unimproved" is their term) land; some will talk to you, however, if you have your complete financial package ready to go (see chapter 16). Be aware, though, that such factors as a property's soil, slope, prevailing winds, water flow or wetlands, and other environmental considerations may affect or alter your original design so that it better fits a chosen site.

Search Strategies

Enlisting the services of a real estate professional is one obvious way to start the search for land. People who have listed their property with an agent are already committed to sell. But if you have very specific land needs, there are other ways to approach the hunt when the listings don't seem to yield what you're looking for.

Write a Letter Siobhan, for example, wanted the seemingly impossible: a three-acre house lot,

close to the center of a town full of high-priced real estate. However, she was willing to spend the time to search out a likely parcel, set a firm budget and deal directly with a land owner who had no apparent interest in selling. She shared her dream in a letter to the owner, and was successful in convincing him that she and her family would make good neighbors, and that her best offer was a fair one. She also had a real estate friend who advised her well. Many people would never take the time to unearth a seller in this fashion; it is a strategy for the determined optimist. Sometimes, as in Siobhan's case, it works. She now has a beautiful home on a secluded lot that would still be unavailable without the extra effort she was willing to make.

One of the reasons Siobhan got her land at a good price was her willingness to see through a thicket of brambles and brush. Other sellers might have offered property more prepared for building;

she was willing to do this work herself, and the final price reflected her initiative about taking on the difficult work of site clearing and preparation.

Place an Ad To find her twenty-six acres, Kathe Higgins advertised in a local newspaper indicating her interest in purchasing land in the town where she finally found her parcel. The ad ran for months, but she eventually got a phone call from the woman who held the property she now owns. With a design and site already in her mind, Kathe loved the property's steep topography and could visualize her house on the hill. The price was right, and she had available cash. The deal was struck.

When Affordable is Less Than Perfect Land far off the beaten track – such as Patti's or Lizabeth's – is usually much less costly than building-ready lots near cities and business centers. Both women value their privacy and natural surroundings, so

their choices worked. However, if you need to be closer to civilization for any one of a number of reasons — job, children or health care needs, for example — you will probably have to do a lot of looking, and a lot of homework, to find land that is both affordable and buildable. Finding the right spot will be an investment of your time in thinking about what you really need, really want, and are willing to pay for the satisfaction of a personal space of your own design.

Lisa Hawkins makes an excellent observation. "Once you know what you can afford, you may find that the most desirable lots in the best locations are out of reach for you financially. But sometimes you can find a lot that is less expensive because it slopes or has setbacks that limit the size of the house. Years ago, a friend of mine on a limited budget found a steeply sloping lot. She hired a young architect who designed a Japanese-style house. My friend had visited Japan and was impressed with the architecture and the fact that households there make do with a lot less space than we in the West are used to. So her home design was essentially one large room suspended above the hillside. The bathroom was the only room with walls. The bedroom was partitioned by attractive folding screens, the living room was defined by a hanging steel fireplace, the dining room by table and chairs. The kitchen ran along one wall by the entry door. To save space, the furnace hung under the house. To reach the house, a stone-flagged path led down from the parking space, planted in Japanese style with a stone lantern lighting the way."

"She had no sooner finished the house than someone offered her double what she had spent for the land and the building. The house was simple, beautiful and suited its site perfectly. So when realtors tell you that you must have three bedrooms, a two-car garage, etc., don't listen. When the time comes, your perfect spot may take a little longer to sell, but someone will love it. Both houses I designed before the current one had only two bedrooms, but the people who bought them loved them, and changed them to suit themselves.

Learn about Buying Land The process of finding and buying a piece of property can be time-consuming, and the most satisfied buyer is an informed one. There are several good books on the topic that can help, listed in Credits and Sources, page 164.

PAPER TIGER

UNLESS YOU ARE BUILDING with cash on hand, you need to approach a lender for financing your project. An addition or renovation can be financed with a home improvement or home equity loan, or with refinancing of your existing mortgage. Building a house requires a different kind of bank product – what's known as a construction loan.

Because the construction loan is essentially uncollateralized – that is, there is no structure with inherent value already on the property – the bank will scrutinize the financial health and credit history of the construction borrower more carefully than it will vet a customer for a mortgage. In addition, the bank will want to see your plans, your building schedule, all the cost estimates for the project and be comfortable that the house will be built to the specifications you have indicated.

"A banker is looking for what I call 'the three Cs'," says Patsy Hennin. "That means, commitment, competence and cash." Patsy co-founded Shelter Institute with her husband, Pat, in 1974. They have taught thousands of amateurs to design, finance and build their own homes, and hear from many students around the country about bankers who balk at the prospect of an owner-built house.

"A bank needs evidence that you have the resources – financial ability, plus the right set of skills – and the determination to see a project through. They need actual proof."

"Bankers are a fairly conservative group, so if you are building for the first time, it may take a lot more preparation to effectively 'sell' your project," says Patsy. "But don't be discouraged if the first bank says no. If you've pre-

THINK LIKE A GIRL SCOUT!

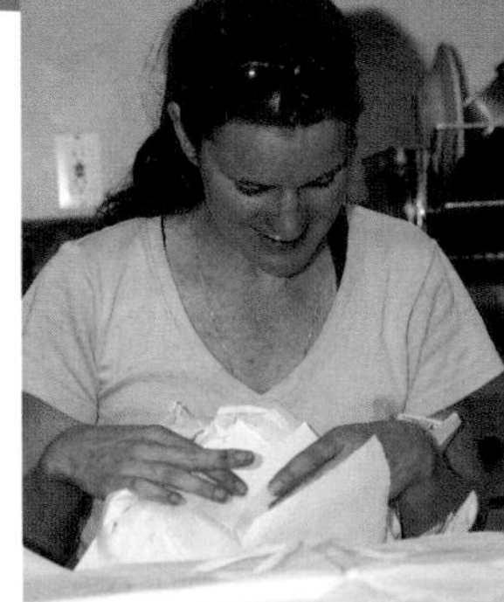

Whether you are building a new house or renovating an existing home, you will collect a lot of paper during the process. Be prepared.

Keep a large accordion file or thick D-ring binder for all of the documents related to the financing and permitting of your project. While building, store these in a secure location for visits made by bank and building inspectors.

WHAT BANKS WANT

Before you meet with a bank about financing, assemble the following:

- Deed, or purchase and sale contract (land)
- Complete plans
- A model, for visual effect (see page 144)
- A timeline for building, fairly specific
- List of specifications and materials, with cost estimates
- Two years of tax returns

Patsy Hennin notes that owner/builders should add twenty-five percent to the estimated bottom line to allow for overruns and any unexpected cost increases.

pared yourself for the process, someone will eventually say yes." She advises many students to try local savings and loans, rather than large commercial banks.

"It's also good if you can buy your land first. Then you can take time to get to know it, maybe clear it yourself and have your parcel as the down payment for your construction loan. Since the permitting process can be lengthy in some areas, you will have time to get your ducks in a row."

Good financial standing, a piece of land, or existing equity in the home you own now can all be proof of the 'cash' C," says Patsy. "To prove competence, you need to show completed plans, a materials list with a cost estimate and an estimate for the cost of labor, even if you will be providing some or all of it. Having a timeline for the work is also a good idea."

In their design/build courses, Patsy and her husband teach students to make cardboard models of their designs. "This is a very good way to impress a lender. Often, people have trouble visualizing a design, even when you show them plans. This is especially true if your design does not resemble the commodity-style projects that banks are used to seeing from developers. A model gives them a very clear picture of your intent; the fact that you've gone to the trouble to show your project so concretely also reinforces their sense of your commitment." Patsy smiles. "If they're unimpressed with all your work, it's time to find another bank."

The Jill Factor

"Depending upon where you live, you may find that being a woman makes it harder to find a

patsy hennin's guide

The design process for a house is often four steps: (1) a prioritized checklist; (2) a detailed set of drawings; (3) a cardboard model and (4) a framing model once the choices of size, shape and framing on-center-spacing have been decided upon. Whether you design the house yourself or buy a set of plans, be sure you create a cardboard model to see the 3-D version of the house and envision where you are going. This exercise will help you check the aesthetics of the building's proportions, the windows, and the size of roof overhang. You can use the model as a tool to verify solar gain through the windows, to check passive solar without over-heating. If this model is done well, it helps secure financing, permits, and mostly gives you a comfort level that you will like the way your house looks and functions.

Materials: Architect's scale, steel framing square, pencil, foam-core mat board, utility knife, cutting mat or board, hot-melt glue gun, scaled plans, straight pins.

Begin with the architect's scale reading dimensions on the ¼ inch=1 foot scale from your plans and allow the scale to do the work of converting to the ⅜ inch=1 foot on the cardboard. This scale allows enough cardboard to give good detail of windows and overhangs on roofs without being too large to transport. The first floor is cut to be the size of the outside of the house (e.g., 24 by 36 feet). Next, each of the walls is cut allowing for the thickness of the cardboard so that, when assembled, they fit together on top of the floor. Usually I cut down the gable end walls to fit between the front and back walls. Before gluing walls together, cut out window openings for each wall, being accurate about the size, shape, placement and height above floor. Using straight pins at corners, assemble before gluing to be sure this design works, or try several versions of each wall. This is a good time to check solar gain with a flashlight at the various times of the year at different times of the day. Get good solar data for Altitude and Azimuth for your latitude (one source is found at www.shelterinstitute.com//tips/truesouth.htm). Optimally your overhang would block summer sun, which is higher in the sky, from hitting the floor, and allow winter sun to fully illuminate the floor for good passive solar gain. When satisfied, glue the windowed walls to the floor and each other. I glue the inside partitions permanently to the first floor and make the second floor and roof removable so we can see inside. The roof is glued to hold its shape with small interior cardboard gussets to maintain the angle of the roof.

sympathetic banker's ear," says Patsy. "Some guys simply won't believe that a woman can do this. In fact, women do it all the time. But for some lenders it will be a brand-new wrinkle."

Sometimes, a woman will need to be creative. Patsy tells a story about a former student who lives in the rural heartland. She tried borrowing for construction from every bank in her area, but they all turned her down, even though she already owned land, and had all her plans and paperwork in order.

"Instead of getting mad or giving up," says Patsy, "she found another way."

The woman placed an advertisement in the paper looking for a balloon loan for two years, with her land as collateral; she offered to pay a competitive interest rate. Her plan was to get a conventional mortgage as soon as the house was built, and pay off the balloon lender.

The strategy worked; a woman with assets to invest read the ad, liked the deal and made the loan. When the woman/builder finished her house on time and on budget, she was able to get a mortgage and pay back her investor.

"That's the meaning of the 'commitment' C," says Patsy. "You have to believe in your project."

Construction Loan Payouts, and Getting a Mortgage

Banks do not immediately pay out all of the funds for construction; each disbursement is contingent on certain benchmarks for the process: completed foundation, completed frame, plumbing and electrical rough-in. And the bank will set the benchmarks. Thus, staying on time and on budget is critical to getting the money you need to pay suppliers and subs, when you need it.

When the project is completed to the bank's satisfaction, a homeowner can get a conventional mortgage for the property, because the collateral for a mortgage – the house – now exists. Sometimes a bank is willing to create a hybrid product, called a convertible loan, that will automatically turn the construction debt into mortgage debt on project completion. Check with your lender about this option, as it means less time-consuming paper- and footwork needed to apply for and secure the two different kinds of financing.

Permits and Inspections

Although they differ from state to state and town to town, most areas of the country subject new construction to the rigors of building codes – standards of construction that insure a measure of integrity to the final product.

Seeing that the codes are adhered to is the job of the CEO – code enforcement officer – or building inspector, who will grant permits for work to begin, then inspect the work so that the process may continue. While many towns and cities have inspectors and building departments to watchdog local construction, this is not universal. There are some places where you can still build what you want, without a permit, any way you choose. In some states, code inspection is only available through a department in the state capital, and not rigorously enforced.

Nevertheless, building a home to meet code requirements, for its site, foundation, frame, roof structure, plumbing, electrical and other key elements is, in fact, a safeguard for the builder, and for future owners. While it's no guarantee that the work meets the highest quality standards, what "building to code" means is that your structure meets the basic requirements for the safety and integrity of its components at the time that it is constructed.

Meet the Building Inspector

Patty Jacobs was a contractor/builder for many years, and at a time when many building professionals would be ready to retire, she decided to take her expertise and translate it into a new job — as a building inspector. Now in her sixties, Patty is one of two women in the fifty-person building department in Las Vegas, Nevada. Here is some advice from one who knows:

"Building Departments are government agencies and as such, are not inherently helpful. They're supposed to be, and the City of Las Vegas does its best to be helpful to owner/builders. We have to assume that the owner/builder knows what she is doing. We can't run jobs for people. We can only guide them superficially and tell them what they can expect in upcoming inspections (what inspectors will look for during the inspection). So this means that before going to the permit department, the owner/builder has all her engineered plans in hand, all the specifications and all the architectural plans also complete. Most building departments will want energy calculations and electrical plans, as well as plumbing and mechanical (for heating and air conditioning).

"So if we are talking about building from the ground up, there is a lot of prep work before going for a permit. Warning: playing stupid, uninformed or ignorant of the building process will get the novice builder no advantage. It's better to read up on construction, visit some construction sites where they are building the kind of building you propose to build, go to the National Association of Women in Construction (www.nawic.org) Web site to pick those women's brains. In other words, be as prepared as you can before venturing in to the permit department.

"Depending on the locale, some small building departments have the plans check and building inspector as a single person — this is good, in order to build a relationship with him/her. It is bad, however, if this person is swamped with work, as most building departments are.

"It is not necessary to know all the building codes to build a house. However, whoever draws your plans should be intimately familiar with the International Residential Code and various local amendments thereto. Also the National Electrical Code (NEC) and International Association of Plumbing and Mechanical Officials (IAPMO) who publish the accepted plumbing and mechanical codes.

"The positive side of the building permit/inspection process is the guarantee that the building that is being built for you is safe and meets current codes. Most building departments are named "Building and Safety" because our primary purpose is to make sure there are no life safety issues in the building — the finished product, as well as the process. Building inspectors check various stages of construction (most, if not all, of which will be covered up post-inspection) to make sure there are no mistakes, omissions and dangerous construction errors. When an inspector signs her name on a permit card that the work is satisfactory, there is a huge responsibility assumed by the inspector and the department. Building inspectors make mistakes too and most building permits will have fine print somewhere saying that the inspectors and/or the department are not responsible for items which may have been overlooked. It happens.

"Most inspectors I know will go on a jobsite with a professional approach and will answer questions regarding the particular inspection. For instance, building inspections are logical, starting from the ground up and from the outside in. Therefore a footing inspection and preslab (if not a raised-floor foundation) would come first. Now if that footing inspection was called and the inspector went out to inspect the footing, the builder might not know that an underslab plumbing inspection and underground electrical inspection should have preceded the footing inspection. This happens to me all the time. I explain the process and advise the builder what I will be looking for on those underslab inspections and also what a footing inspection entails. To me this is just being courteous and informative, but my patience will wear thin if the builder continues to pepper me with questions which obviously tells me that she hasn't got the foggiest idea what inspection is all about.

"I work for a department that gives us cell phones to use so we can make calls, but incoming calls are blocked. So I carry a personal cell phone and always give the number to builders and superintendents. I want them to call me with questions, have the ability to call and cancel an inspection, or find out a window of time for the inspection. This saves me a lot of trouble. However, I don't like getting calls at 8 p.m. on a Saturday night to talk about a job. My work hours are 6:30 a.m to 3:30 p.m. Monday through Friday, and if you have questions about your job, please call during those hours. I usually have to train owner/builders because they forget that the building inspectors have other jobsites besides theirs. (I just went through this myself, as I did a major remodel on my house, which is taking FOREVER to finish!)"

What to Expect

Depending on where and what you want to build, the process of getting the site ready for building and then raising the structure can be fairly simple, or long and complex. If you've bought a parcel with well and waste disposal systems (septic) installed, or municipal water and sewer in place, the site is just about ready for the house. Usually, though, that's not the case. You have bought a raw piece of land and need a well and septic tank and field, or municipal water and sewage hookup.

As a point of departure, here is a listing of documents needed and inspections required for building a house in a semi-rural, high property value town in southeastern New York. It will explain, by its detail and length, why checking first with the building department is a good idea. It is also one of the most rigorous processes anyone building a house might encounter — a worst-case scenario — so don't let it scare you!

Permits Required

- building permit
- blasting/fill site work (if needed)
- tree cutting permit (if trees will be cut down)
- electrical
- plumbing
- HVAC (heating, ventilation, air-conditioning)
- Board of Health permitting for septic field
- a permit from the Highway Department for a new driveway

Paper to File with Building Department

- building permit application
- three copies of the property survey
- three copies of the plot (site) plan, prepared by a licensed engineer or surveyor
- residential site plan determining lot coverage (to comply with a local ordinance to prevent oversized houses)
- copy of the contractor's home improvement license
- three sets of plans and specifications, prepared or certified by a licensed professional
- certificate of workman's compensation benefits for any employees

Inspections must be done in a specific sequence. Obviously, if you are using subs to do some of the work, the inspection of one sub's work must be completed before the next sub arrives to complete the next part of the sequence. It is a scheduling challenge, to say the least.

Inspection Sequence

- footings inspection (inspect forms and soil)
- before backfill of the foundation; inspect waterproofing and exterior drains
- before slab is poured; check gravel, vapor barrier and reinforcement
- framing inspection
- rough electrical
- rough plumbing
- rough HVAC
- fireplace inspection (three inspections for masonry, three for modular fireplaces)
- insulation
- Sheetrock (before taping)
- final plumbing test
- smoke detector test
- final building inspection
- final electrical inspection
- final health department inspection for septic system
- well driller's report

Ta-da! File for Certificate of Occupancy; when it is issued, you can move in.

Instructions and Resources

BUILDING LESSONS

UNLESS YOU'RE ALREADY a practiced do-it-herselfer or construction professional, to feel confident and empowered you will first need to get comfortable with the tools and techniques of building.

The best learning experiences get you involved. If your class or workshop shows tools, but doesn't let you use them, be wary. You might want to talk to people who have taken the course you're interested in. Lee McBride, whom I met at Yestermorrow, had this to say about her week at the Carpentry for Women workshop:

"A woman in the class told us that she had signed up for a women's carpentry class in Connecticut, but when she got there, the instructor told her she couldn't use the power equipment. For insurance reasons, he would *demonstrate* the power tools while students *watched*. So why pay hundreds of dollars to take a class that just as easily could have been presented in a $19.95 video tape? She quit in disgust. In contrast, the Yestermorrow class is all about getting your hands dirty – owning the knowledge and developing the confidence that comes from hands-on experience. I went home afterward and saw my house in a completely different way. I listed all the things that could be done and was able to categorize them as hard, easy, short-term, long-term, do-it-yourself, and hire a professional. Before, I couldn't tell which was which."

So, *caveat emptor*. But here are some opportunities that we've already checked out.

Home Centers

Recognizing that women buy half the hardware sold in their stores, the major home center chains now actively entice their women customers with learning opportunities. Many give regular evening and weekend workshops for women who want to learn basic skills: laying tile, painting, minor plumbing and wiring installations, using power tools, and more. The help desk at most of these outlets will usually post a list of classes available to their customers. They are free; signup is often required, though some workshops wel-

come walk-ins. Always ask if the classes are demonstrations or hands-on opportunities.

Do Well by Doing Good

Habitat for Humanity's Women Build program is an excellent way to learn building skills in the company of other women. You don't need any construction experience to volunteer your time; all you need is the desire to help another woman and her family construct a simple, decent, affordable place to live (see "With a Little Help From Her Friends," chapter 3).

Women Build was designed for women who've always wanted to help build houses, but hesitated to sign up with Habitat's regular crews, which are often dominated by men who have professional or significant do-it-yourself experience. On a Women Build project, you can learn every aspect of house building, from pouring a foundation to finish carpentry, in a collaborative, supportive environment where women with skills work side by side with newcomers. Everyone feels empowered by the process.

To find out more about Women Build, go to www.habitat.org/wb. You will find current listings for projects throughout the United States and around the world; most Habitat chapters list all their contact information online, so it's easy to find a project in progress in your area. If your local Habitat chapter has not yet sponsored a Women Build house, perhaps your interest and willingness to make it happen will get one going!

Design/Build Schools

You can also develop building skills with an education vacation. A number of design/build schools around the United States and Canada offer weekend, one- or two-week courses in designing, building, basic carpentry and other trade skills. Some courses are created specifically for women and taught by female building professionals. All instruction offers hands-on projects to hone real-world skills.

Even if you intend to hire professionals to complete your house or home improvement, an intensive course in design and building will provide you with the knowledge and vocabulary to work comfortably with architects and contractors. When you consider that a house costs upwards of $100 per square foot to build – that's a simple house; custom details will make the bill much higher – the investment of a thousand dollars or so to learn building basics is money well spent. Your conversations with your builder will no longer feel like a struggle to understand someone who speaks another language!

Inside a hangar-like work space, a small building goes up, designed and constructed by students at Shelter Institute's Small House workshop.

In addition to Yestermorrow Design/Build School (www.yestermorrow.org or phone 802-496-5545; see Building 101, chapter 12), here are some other programs that offer excellent, woman-friendly courses:

Shelter Institute, Woolwich, Maine

The Hennin family – Pat, Patsy, sons Raoul and Gaius, daughter Blueberry, plus a few grandchildren – operates the longest established design/build school in the country. Since 1974, more than 30,000 students, ages sixteen to seventy-six, have attended their one-, two- and three-week courses. The Hennins are post-and-beam, timber- frame specialists, offering pre-cut timber-frame kits and custom designs as well as classes.

A recent addition to their design/build offerings is a one-week Small House Building Class, during which students will collaborate on design, and construct a small (10- by 16-foot) house – perfect for the woman who'd like to create her own cozy cottage. It's a great opportunity to experience the building process in a small-scale, hands-on way – start to finish.

Weekend classes in specialized topics are also available throughout the year, including a Contract-It-Yourself workshop to assist those who want to act as general contractors for their home or improvement.

Set on a beautiful sixty-eight-acre campus on the Maine coast, Shelter Institute also houses a fabulous tool shop and bookstore where anyone interested in home design and building arts could happily spend a day. You will find a huge selection of books and tools here that you'd be hard-pressed to find anywhere else under one roof, including a wide assortment of women-friendly Japanese saws and hammers.

For course dates and further information, visit www.shelterinstitute.com, or phone 207-442-7938

Heartwood School, Washington, Massachusetts

Offering two-week courses in homebuilding, a variety of courses in timber framing (in conjunction with the Timber Framers Guild) and a one-week course in carpentry for women, Heartwood also provides lots of hands-on experience to its students. Located in the Berkshire Hills of western Massachusetts, Heartwood is another opportunity to learn building skills in beautiful surroundings. In addition to building courses, there are also specialized courses in various aspects of woodworking, as well as classes in furniture-making. Co-directors and founders Will and Michele Beemer have been shepherding homebuilders and carpenters-in-training through the hurdles of hands-on learning since 1978, so the program is well-honed by their experience.

The women's carpentry class is taught by professional female contractors, and helps women build the skills they need to complete their own projects, or even strike out on a new career in the construction trade.

Contact www.heartwoodschool.com, or phone 413-623-6677 for dates and information.

Power Tool Savvy

Short on time, but eager to learn? If you live near California's central coast, Mz. Fix-itz™ can come to you.

Four years ago, Mary Martin moved from the San Francisco area to the central coast and began buying, renovating and selling fixer-upper properties. She had spent 1996–97 in Costa Rica, where she had overcome her fear of power tools and built a cabin for herself; without those skills, she could not have earned a living with her real estate ventures.

With the purchase – from its original owner – of a '64 Chevy pickup truck, Mary found she had everything she needed to hire herself out between fixups for decorating and what she calls "handy-ma'am" projects.

"That was the start of Mz. Fix-itz," recalls Mary. I sat at my desk one evening trying to come up with a name that captured the essence of what I do and who I am."

"Most of my clients were females who wanted to watch me as I worked on simple tasks: changing light fixtures, installing closet rods, and the like. I explained to them that these were things they could do for themselves, but most expressed fear of power tools or some other internal obstacle. That was when I got the idea of having a power tool workshop designed expressly for women."

"When I approached a local female hardware store manager with my idea, she thought it was great and said she'd support me if I wanted to run workshops at her store. The first one was held in November of 2002. In April 2003 I invested in a mobile van, painted it with my logo – Rosie the Riveter's body and my face – and took my workshops on the road."

Mary's workshops empower women with the basics of power tool operation, safety, and uses. Motivating, inspiring and confidence building, the ninety-minute workshop is designed to get women started on doing their own home-repairing and

improvement projects. Because the workshop is mobile, it can go anywhere and be set up in just thirty minutes.

For more information, contact Mz. Fix-itz at www.mzfixitz.com, or phone 805-610-1789.

More Lessons

When research for this book began, a search-engine inquiry for "carpentry classes for women" yielded a page or two of sources. Let your computer do the walking; there are now dozens of offerings throughout the United States, Canada and the world. But check before you leap; make sure the courses offer hands-on instruction. Female instructors will also make the experience less intimidating; find out who's teaching the class, how many such workshops she's taught, and if there are any references you can check (especially if the course costs more than $50.)

Many community colleges and continuing education programs offer courses in general contracting, how to build your own house and other building topics. The best are taught by professionals; a general contractor will take you through the steps of contracting the building of a house. You may want a recommendation from a former student before you plunk down your cash. A good instructor can give you a basic outline of the process that can help you structure your own project. A poor teacher may leave you more confused.

GREAT BOOKS ABOUT HOME MAKING

There are some wonderful narratives about homebuilding that go into detail, not only about the nails-and-lumber basics, but also about the many personal, financial and emotional ups-and-downs of the process. Anyone contemplating owner/builder-ship should read one and all.

- Noted architect/academic/nonfiction writer Witold Rybczynski set out to design and construct a little shelter on country property where he could build a boat. Gradually, this plan changed shape and turned into a house for himself and his wife, Shirley Hallam. Fortunately for all of us, he documents the metamorphosis in *The Most Beautiful House in the World* (paperback, Penguin Books, reprint ed. 1990). You'll find the process well-explained from a variety of perspectives: personal, historical and metaphysical, as well as architectural. A fascinating read.

- Author Michael Pollan decided to build a writing house on his property, with almost no do-it-yourself experience and (by his own admission) no talent in that direction. *A Place of My Own: The Education of an Amateur Builder* (paperback, Delta/Dell, 1997), Pollan's discovery of his inner carpenter, is wonderfully encouraging to the novice. You will definitely emerge from this book with a feeling that, "If he could manage this project, there's a lot of hope for me."

- Tracy Kidder's *House* (paperback, Mariner Books, 1999) chronicles a more typical scenario. The owner/builders hire an architect and a contractor to build their dream house; Kidder observes the process and interaction of this sometimes contentious triangle as they proceed from plans to move-in day. If you haven't read this best-seller, don't hesitate. It's an indispensable book for anyone contemplating building — although costs have certainly escalated since the Souweine family had their home constructed in the 1980s.

Getting the Right Stuff

THE MATERIAL WORLD

The cost of lumber is one of the biggest expenses of homebuilding. Make friends with the folks at your local lumberyard. Ask lots of questions; learn about the various grades and types of wood. Ask for builders' discounts on your quantity orders. The lumber you see stacked here has been "stickered"—1- by 1-inch stock is placed perpendicularly between layers of board to separate each layer so that air can circulate and the wood does not become moldy or discolored by moisture. Use the same technique when stacking lumber at your building site.

THERE'S NO DOUBT ABOUT IT. Building materials are expensive, and getting more so.

No matter how much sweat equity – your own labor – you apply to your project, you will have to buy materials.

This chapter is a little scrapbook of ideas for saving money – particularly in the fixture and finish details – that the homeowners in this book used to cut the final costs of their projects. You can use some of their ideas, or search out your own. Happy bargain hunting!

Tile Ideas

Ceramic tile is a fairly cost-effective floor, wall and countertop treatment. Creating a pattern using two or more colors is one strategy to get more design impact for your dollar.

The pictures on these pages show other techniques to achieve a custom look for less.

Above and top right: Mosaic tile squares make a costly overall floor treatment; using just a few in an interesting pattern dresses up Siobhan's first-floor bathroom; in the master bath shower, two handpainted tiles in a mosaic "frame" dress up an otherwise inexpensive and plain white tile treatment.

Alison also created a beautiful, abstract design for her bathroom floor using broken Mexican saltillo tile seconds—very inexpensive. Her radiant floor heat makes them feel as warm as they look!

Alison bought glass block cheaply at an architectural salvage store and used it to create a light window in the wall partition between the main open section of her house and the bathroom. She surrounded the block with a mosaic she designed with small bits of salvaged tile, arranged in an attractive geometric pattern.

Granite is a popular and expensive countertop material; practically indestructible, it is coveted for kitchen surfaces. Instead of paying $100 a foot, Lizabeth and her tape measure found a remnant that would perfectly fit the counter in her kitchen: score!

Right: Lizabeth saved hundreds of dollars on the cost of her hardwood (yellow birch) floors by using the short ends left over from customers who like 8- to 12-foot strip lengths. Her floors are laid with 2-, 3-, 4-, and occasionally 5-foot strips. "It was a bigger layout job, but well worth our extra labor," says Lizabeth.

Leftovers

If you sew, you know that the best buys in a fabric store are the last couple of yards left on a bolt — the remnants.

Building suppliers also have remnants, and are usually willing to part with them for a song. Always ask about the leftovers of a material you like; you might find a real deal.

Great Stuff, Less Money. Wouldn't you love a whirlpool tub? A gorgeous custom sink fabricated in a beautiful material? Wouldn't we all? Lizabeth purchased her whirlpool tub and bath hardware from a discount plumbing supply catalog. Closeouts and discontinued models are often a fraction of the original price.

Lizabeth didn't even need to scout for the countertop that fits perfectly next to the stove; it was the piece cut out from her main counter for the drop-in sink.

Sinks fabricated in exotic metals are the rage; Morgan purchased hers for about a third of the cost of the custom sinks you see in decorating magazines. Here's her story: "My sink came from a wonderful little family business in Ohio that has been making copper kettles for over a hundred years. They actually knocked a few dollars off the price because I didn't want the kettle with handles. I had the drain hole cut at a local machine shop, and ordered the brass sink plug unit from a plumbing supply store". *See product info in Credits and Sources.*

Morgan's beautiful handmade door deserves its custom latch and hinges. Wrought by a local blacksmith from Morgan's own design, they are a signature element of her home's personality.

Little Luxuries

Details make a difference. Sometimes you will find a beautiful bargain, but often, the money you save on other items – or just having a smaller house to finish – will afford the details that make your house special. Here are a few finishing touches to appreciate.

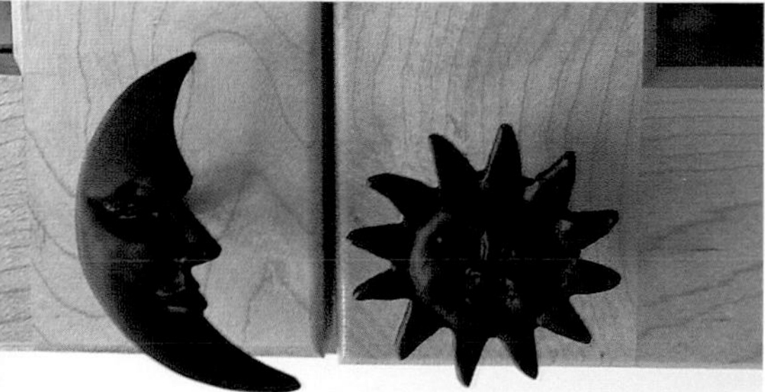

Lizabeth and Skip dressed up their stock cabinets with decorative hardware in a variety of motifs: sun, moon, stars and animals. The hardware was inexpensive, but gives a custom flourish to the kitchen.

Siobhan's family loves a fire in the evening; she didn't want the mess or worry of a fire-place. The compromise: a gas fireplace in the great room that's on instantly, requires no cleanup and is a perfect backup heater for chilly evenings when the furnace is not turned on.

Left: Morgan's garden fence and lattice are her own design; she even made the rustic latch and hand-wrought wooden hinges.

credits & sources

All photography is by Karen Leffler unless otherwise noted.

Introduction—

p. 10: photos by Cathy Hays; p. 11 photo courtesy of Laurie Ardison and Tracy Vaughan.

For those who would like to explore the inner significance of home – its deeper and more personal meanings – I suggest Clare Cooper Marcus' *House as a Mirror of Self* (paperback; Conari Press, 1995).

Chapter 1: Southern Comfort, New England Style

Snapshots: Nicole Rossi

Siobhan is very grateful to her mother and her father-in-law, who never saw the finished house, but were very encouraging to her and her husband about having a house of their own. "Their spirits were very much with us as we built it," says Siobhan.

She also thanks her friends: Michael Crandley, who helped along her carpentry skills, and Michael's wife, Donna, who is a contractor and provided Siobhan with lots of pointers on maintaining good communication with subcontractors and keeping the work flowing.

Lemon tree wall mural (p. 23) painted by Blair MacLeod, through Tile America, New Haven, Connecticut.

Chapter 2: A Dream in the Desert

Custom kitchen iron work was crafted by Tom Stengel at Desert Iron, 435-259-1170.

In addition to all the friends who assisted her at her work parties, Alison thanks her good friends and neighbors Dave Focardi and Jenny Weidersee – "seems to me, looking back, they were just always there to help when I needed it. Also, Arthur Pitari, a good friend and skilled builder from New Orleans, flew out to lend a hand for ten days when I was really having trouble staying focused. He was a great teacher; from him I learned how to lay glass bricks, install gutters, put panes of glass in doors and frame walls."

For more information about Alison's earth-friendly building material, read *Earthbag Building: The Tools, Tricks, and Techniques* (paperback, New Society, 2004), written by Alison's friends, Kaki Hunter and Dan Kiffmeyer.

Alison's business, Canyon Springs Consulting, counsels owner/builders, as well as women-owned and operated businesses, alisonlara@frontiernet.net

Chapter 3: With a Little Help from Her Friends

Regular volunteers on a Women Build project have the opportunity to learn important building and carpentry skills, as well as an understanding of the *sequence* of steps that combine to finish a house.

An excellent reference, *How to Build a House* (Taunton, 2002), written by longtime carpenter and Habitat volunteer Larry Haun, provides a look at how a basic Habitat house is built, with plenty of good tips for any potential home maker – especially one who is building on a tight budget.

For a great overview of the international reach of Habitat for Humanity International, read Habitat co-founder Millard Fuller's book, *A Simple, Decent Place to Live*, (hardcover, Word, 1995).

Chapter 4: Vermont Two-Step

Snapshots: Lizabeth, Skip, and friends.

Learn more about Lizabeth and Skip's heating system. *The Book of Masonry Stoves: Rediscovering an Old Way of Warming* by David Lyle (paperback: Energy Shelter, 1998), offers lots of details.

Masonry heater for the Moniz/Dewhirst house by Temp-Cast (www.tempcast.com).

For more about timber-frame houses, visit the Web site for the Timber Framers Guild, www.tfguild.org, for postings about timber-frame classes and workshops, as well as a bookstore where you can order books and videos about timber framing.

Chapter 5: Building a Community

There are cohousing communities worldwide. To find out more and see listings, visit the web site of the nonprofit Cohousing Association of the United States (Coho/US) at www.cohousing.org.

Chapter 7: Resourceful Ranch

All snapshots, Lisa Hawkins, except p. 70, Sarah Holland.

For design help, Lisa strongly recommends *Homing Instinct*, by John Connell (paperback, McGraw-Hill, 1998) — a great "first book" for those serious about designing and building their own homes. Connell talks you through the process like a good friend and mentor. He is the founder of Yestermorrow Design/Build School.

In the late nineteenth century, pioneers in the Nebraska sand hills had no access to trees for building. What they did have was tall grass, which homesteaders harvested and baled, and made into walls for their houses. Many of these early homes are still standing today, a testament to the viability of this earth-friendly building method.

There are many books about building with straw bales, including *The New Strawbale Home* by Catherine Wanek (hardcover, Gibbs Smith, 2003).

Chapter 8: The House That Jill Renovated

Snapshots: Jill MacNaughton

In addition to scrutinizing dozens of books and magazines for ideas she liked, Jill MacNaughton recommends *Home Renovation* by Francis D.K. Ching and Dale Miller (paperback, Van Nostrand Reinhold, 1983). "It is a great book loaded with drawings indicating all the measurements beginners need to know," says Jill.

Chapter 9: Up a Mountain

Snapshot: Kathe Higgins.

Kathe expresses her gratitude to her parents — "their financial help kept me from falling off the precipice so that I could keep my home" — and the dozens of subcontractors and suppliers who provided all kinds of good advice. She is especially appreciative of her workmen, Mike Putnam and Rocky Daniels, who stuck with her through the roughest part of her journey.

Kathe's ironwork dining table and chairs, candlesticks, and coffee table base, all handcrafted by Iron Horse Metal Works, Bristol, New Hampshire; www.ironhorsemetalworks.com.

Butterfly bench from Cricket Forge, Durham, North Carolina; www.cricketforge.com

Solar installation by Solar Works; www.solar-works.com.

Chapter 10: His . . .and Hers

Snapshots: Morgan Irons and Alan Paschell.

Clay sculptures by Alan Paschell.

Chapter 11: Pioneers: Twentieth-Century Home Makers

All illustrations for Leila Ross Wilburn, courtesy Agnes Scott College (Wilburn's alma mater) in Atlanta, Georgia.

Linda Gray, Access Services Librarian at the college's McCain Library, lives in a Wilburn-designed house and loves its details. The library will soon put a large collection of Wilburn floor plan drawings and renderings from her original plan books online. A small collection of these books is also available for on-site research at the reference library of the Atlanta History Center.

All images for Helen Nearing are courtesy of the Thoreau Institute at Walden Woods, in Lincoln, Massachusetts.

Part II: A Home Maker's Guide

Photo, p. 111 Kate Stephenson, Yestermorrow Design/Build School

No patent for the first circular saw exists, and accounts of the Babbitt legend vary. However, most stories about its origin credit Sister Tabitha Babbitt, a member of the Harvard, Massachusetts, Shaker community, with designing this ingenious alternative to the two-man pit saw in about 1810. This wonderful invention has spawned many variations, including the light and convenient cordless models available today.

Coincidentally, once they master its control, many women find that it is their favorite tool. Says Alison, "I love it best, not only because it was invented by a woman, but also because I used to be afraid of it — and now I'm not!" Tabitha Babbitt is also credited with the invention of cut (as opposed to hand-forged) nails, making mass production possible and significantly lowering the cost of this building staple..

credits & sources

Chapter 12: Building 101: Learning the Basics

Photo, p 118 & p 119, bottom, Kate Stephenson/Yestermorrow Design/Build School.

Many companies now make work gloves in small sizes to fit a woman's hand — www.womanswork.com is one source for a very nice suede glove; www.shelterinstitute.com stocks many inexpensive varieties in small sizes. For safty goggles with built-in diopters for those who need reading glasses, www.woodcraft.com offers several different strengths.

Chapter 13: Jill's Tool Kit

Japanese hand tools are not always available in big-box hardware stores. Here are some good catalog sources:

- www.shelterinstitute.com
- www.woodcraft.com, web site for Woodcraft (in 36 states, including Hawaii) and Woodworker's Club retail stores, offers an extensive selection of fine tools, for all types of woodworking, including specialized tools for timber framing and fine cabinet work. Get their catalog to browse at your leisure. Woodworker's Club (currently with four outlets) is the only network of do-it-yourself woodworking shops that provide on-site, fully equipped shop space and instructors, as well as ongoing schedules of hands-on classes.
- www.thejapanwoodworker.com is another catalog/web site source offering beautiful hand tools.

One book with great instructions for using many of the tools described in this chapter is *Getting Started in Woodworking* by Aime Ontario Fraser (Taunton, 2003). Aime, a gifted woodworker, writes for many woodworking magazines, has taught at the Wooden Boat school in Brooklin, Maine, and currently gives classes and private lessons at the Woodworker's Club in Norwalk, Connecticut.

Special thanks to John and Ginny Matchak, owners of Woodworker's Club in Norwalk, Connecticut, who graciously loaned power tools for the photos in this chapter.

Chapter 14: The Drawing Board: Making a Design

A good place to begin is *Building Construction Illustrated* by Francis D.K. Ching and Cassandra Adams (paperback, Wiley, 2000).

Snapshot, p. 137, Kaki Hunter.

Chapter 15: The Right Spot: Finding and Buying Land

Finding and Buying Your Place in the Country by Les Scher and Carol Scher (Dearborn Trade Publishing, 1992) is an excellent resource. For an examination of environmental issues related to land and existing homes, read *The Home and Land Buyer's Guide to the Environment* by Barry Chalofsky (paperback, Center for Urban Policy Research, 1997).

Chapter 16; Paper Tiger: Finanacing, Permits and Inspections

Photo p. 144, Shelter Institute.

Estimating Home Building Costs by W.P. Jackson (paperback, Craftsman Publishing, 1982) is a good basic handbook for figuring the costs of everything needed for constructing a home.

Find out which codes are followed in your area, then read the appropriate guide or handbook. These are expensive; check the local library for the most recent editions.

Patty Jacobs, photo, p. 146, David Mason. Thanks to Patty for her insights on the inspection process.

For permit and inspection guidelines special thanks to the building department of the Town of Pound Ridge, New York, building inspector Jim Perry and office manager Charlotte Sasloff.

Chapter 17: Building Lessons: Instructions and Resources

Photo, p. 152, Shelter Institute; p. 154, Mary Martin.

18: The Material World: Getting the Right Stuff

Copper kitchen sink, crafted from a kettle from D. Picking & Co., makers of copper kettles since 1874; 119 South Walnut, Bucyrus, Ohio; 419-562-6891.

Back cover image, center, Kate Stephenson, Yestermorrow Design/Build School.

For more information about women and building, and the homes in this book visit www.thehousethatjillbuilt.com.

acknowledgments

FOR THEIR IMAGINATION, DETERMINATION, AND GENEROSITY in sharing their personal stories, I am deeply grateful to the women whose building experiences have helped create this book. I thank them, and their families, for the cooperation and hospitality extended to us while Karen and I interrupted their busy lives with cameras, questions, and endless calls and e-mails.

I also thank all of the organizations and companies that recognize and honor a woman's power to do-it-herself: Yestermorrow Design/Build School; Shelter Institute; Habitat for Humanity's Women Build program; Mary Martin and her one-woman DIY roadshow; and the Northeast Sustainable Energy Association (NESEA) are just a few among the many who helped me.

All the wonderful people at Gibbs Smith have made publishing this book a joy: Suzanne Taylor, who believed in my proposal; Alison Einerson, who gave it her enthusiastic support; Jennifer Maughan, who carefully guided its editing; Kurt Wahlner, art director and fielder of questions *extraordinaire*; a dedicated and inspired design staff; Christopher Robbins and Dennis Awsumb, whose thoughtful suggestions helped me make it better; and Gibbs himself, who with his gifted team has built a warm and welcoming writers' house.

I thank Kate Braid for the opportunity to share her wonderful poems about the building life. Finally, I offer deepest appreciation to photographer Karen Leffler, whose spirit, talent, good humor, and grasp of this project have made our collaboration an enjoyable and fulfilling one.

An idea in its infancy can be a fragile creature; sometimes it needs a bit of nurturing and support. To my friends and family – especially my husband, children, sisters, and my late father and father-in-law – know that your encouragement has been a constant source of sustenance.

– *Judy Ostrow*

The women in our book inspire feelings of deep appreciation and comradery. As a builder of three hand-made homes, I treasure the spirit that calls us to dream, and then supports us to bring the dream into reality. I have immense respect for the courage and dedication of the home makers in this book – and home makers everywhere.

Thank you, Judy, for inviting me along for this project. I am forever grateful to you, and in love with picture-taking!

– *Karen Leffler*

afterword

The Little Poem

Size is a big thing in construction.
Everything is measured and found wanting—
tools, materials, people.

How big is your hammer?
Is that all?
Don't you have anything heavier?
Is that the best you can do?

After a while I wonder,
couldn't we do as well with smaller parts,
more skill?
Imagine building a tower
with teeny weeny hammers
and a big heart?
There'd be less to throw away
and less to clean.

An itsy bitsy tower would linger near the ground,
smell the daisies.
We'd cut less trees and haul less rock.
Smaller hands,
a woman's perhaps,
could build this very well.
Think how far moonlight could travel
over such a delicate space.

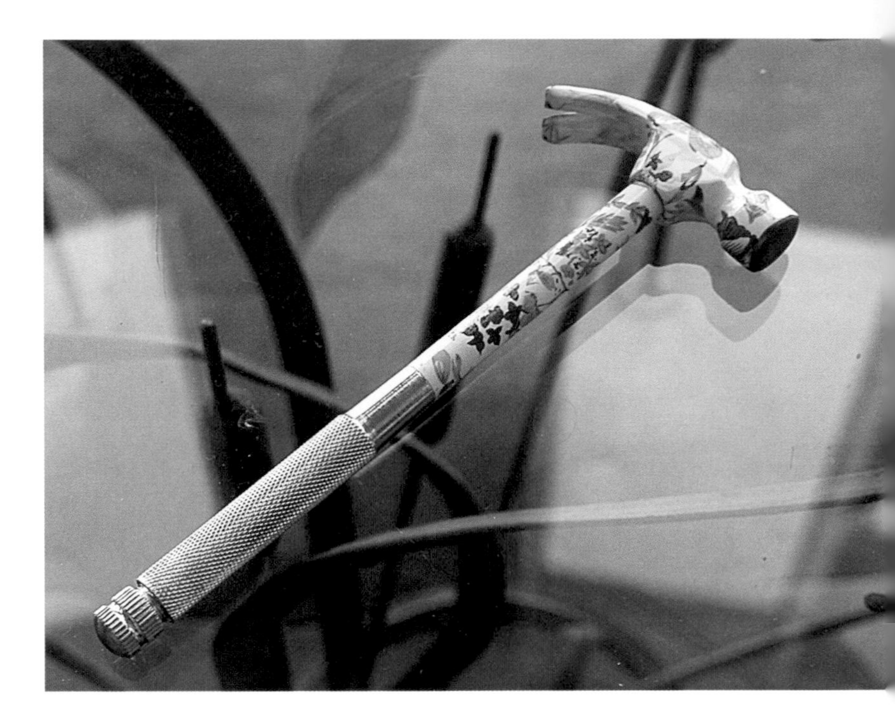

We would have to balance
everything.
With less to make, less to borrow, less to buy
we might spend more time
thinking of little,
dreaming dreams
small enough to put our arms around.

—Kate Braid